# BUGS

*of*

## ONTARIO

### John Acorn

Illustrations by Ian Sheldon

Lone Pine Publishing

The Publisher: Lone Pine Publishing

10145 - 81 Ave.                          1808 – B Street NW, Suite 140
Edmonton, AB  T6E 1W9                     Auburn, WA
Canada                                    USA 98001

Website: http://www.lonepinepublishing.com

National Library of Canadian Cataloguing in Publication Data

Acorn, John Harrison, 1958–
    Bugs of Ontario

    Includes bibliographical references and index.
    ISBN 1-55105-287-3

    1. Insects—Ontario—Identification. I. Title.
QL476.A362003      595.7'097123      C00-910507-7

*Editorial Director:* Nancy Foulds
*Project Editor:* Lee Craig
*Editorial:* Lee Craig, Sandra Bit
*Illustrations Coordinator:* Carol Woo
*Production Manager:* Gene Longson
*Layout & Production:* Lynett McKell
*Book Design:* Robert Weidemann & Heather Markham
*Cover Design:* Gerry Dotto
*Cover Illustration:* Ian Sheldon
*Illustrations:* Ian Sheldon
*Photography:* John Acorn
*Separations & Film:* Elite Lithographers Co.

Many thanks to Great North Productions and photographer Robert van Schaik for the
use of the photo on p. 11.

The illustrations in this book are owned by Ian Sheldon and Lone Pine Publishing.

The illustration on the front cover is the Six-spotted Tiger Beetle.

We acknowledge the financial support of the Government of Canada through the Book
Publishing Industry Development Program (BPIDP) for our publishing activities.

PC: 01

# CONTENTS

# DEDICATION

To my friends at Science North and their wonderful annual Bugfest.

# ACKNOWLEDGEMENTS

Working on this book was a great pleasure, largely thanks to Ian Sheldon, whose superb and accurate paintings brought the bugs of Ontario to life. Ian worked from his own impressive knowledge of arthropods, as well as from slides and specimens, and special thanks go to the Canadian National Collection of Insects and the E.H. Strickland Entomological Museum for allowing us to borrow specimens for reference. Thanks also go to Henri Goulet, who graciously agreed to look over the manuscript for me. The following people also helped by reviewing text and responding to queries: Gary Anweiler, George Ball, Cheryl Barr, Brian Brown, Rob Cannings, Eric Coombs, Ed Fuller, Robert Holmberg, Reuben Kaufman, James LaBonte, Dave Lawrie, David Maddison, Chris Schmidt, Ales Smetana, Felix Sperling, Terry Thormin, Richard Westcott and Daryl Williams. The staff of Lone Pine Publishing have been a pleasure to work with, and I would especially like to recognize Lynett McKell, Gerry Dotto, Lee Craig, Nancy Foulds and Shane Kennedy for their contributions. Finally, I would like to thank Dena Stockburger for her loving support, Jesse and Benjamin Acorn for their perspectives on bugs and life, and my parents for allowing me to be a bugster throughout my childhood—a phase that apparently has not yet ended for me.

**BUTTERFLIES**

Silver-spotted
Skipper, p. 28

Black Swallowtail
p. 29

Eastern Tiger
Swallowtail, p. 30

Cabbage White
p. 31

Clouded Sulphur
p. 32

Spring Azure
p. 33

Great Spangled
Fritillary, p. 34

Pearl Crescent
p. 35

Question Mark
p. 36

Mourning Cloak
p. 37

Painted Lady
p. 38

Red Admiral
p. 39

White Admiral
p. 40

Common Wood
Nymph, p. 41

Monarch
p. 42

Purplish Ghost
Moth, p. 43

**MOTHS**

Rosy Maple Moth
p. 44

Polyphemus Moth
p. 45

Cecropia Moth
p. 46

Luna Moth
p. 47

5

**MOTHS**

Twin-spotted Sphinx, p. 48

Big Poplar Sphinx p. 49

Snowberry Clearwing p. 50

Apple Sphinx p. 51

Waved Sphinx p. 52

Virginia Ctenucha p. 53

Garden Tiger Moth, p. 54

White Underwing, p. 55

Once-married Underwing, p. 56

Spear-marked Black, p. 57

**BEETLES**

Six-spotted Tiger Beetle, p. 58

Caterpillar Hunter p. 59

Purple-rimmed Carabus, p. 60

American Hemispherical Savage Beetle, p. 61

Burying Beetle p. 62

Hairy Rove Beetle p. 63

Pinching Beetle p. 64

Bess Beetle p. 65

Spotted Grape Beetle, p. 66

Hermit Beetle p. 67

Gold-dust Buprestid, p. 68

Eyed Click Beetle p. 69

**BEETLES**

Woods Firefly
p. 70

Goldenrod Soldier
Beetle, p. 71

Red Flat Bark
Beetle, p. 72

Multicoloured Asian
Ladybug, p. 73

Notable Sawyer
p. 74

Locust Borer
p. 75

Dogbane Beetle
p. 76

Bird-poop Weevil
p. 77

**WASPS, ANTS, BEES & SAWFLIES**

Pavement Ant
p. 78

Carpenter Ant
p. 79

Bumblebee
p. 80

Pigeon Horntail
p. 81

Bald-faced Hornet
p. 82

Yellow Jacket
p. 83

Mud Dauber
p. 84

Cicada Killer
p. 85

**TWO-WINGED FLIES**

Cow Killer
p. 86

Stump Stabber
p. 87

Hover Fly
p. 88

Horse Fly
p. 89

**TWO-WINGED FLIES**

Robber Fly
p. 90

Brown Crane Fly
p. 91

Anthrax Beefly
p. 92

Green Lacewing
p. 93

**LACEWINGS & THEIR RELATIVES**

Dobsonfly
p. 94

Mantis Fly
p. 95

Ant Lion
p. 96

Leaf-footed Bug
p. 97

**SUCKING BUGS**

Large Milkweed
Bug, p. 98

Boxelder Bug
p. 99

Green Stink Bug
p. 100

Harlequin Bug
p. 101

Buffalo
Treehopper, p. 102

Candy-stripe
Leafhopper, p. 103

Dog Day Cicada
p. 104

European Earwig
p. 105

European Mantid
p. 106

Walking Stick
p. 107

**GRIGS & THEIR RELATIVES**

Wood Roach
p. 108

Eastern Subterranean
Termite, p. 109

Field Cricket
p. 110

Road Duster
p. 111

Angular-winged
Katydid, p. 112

Northern Mole
Cricket, p. 113

Tree Cricket
p. 114

Ebony Jewelwing
p. 115

Emerald
Spreadwing, p. 116

Boreal Bluet
p. 117

Sedge Sprite
p. 118

Green Darner
p. 119

Canada Darner
p. 120

Rusty Snaketail
p. 121

American Emerald
p. 122

Common Whitetail
p. 123

Yellow-legged
Meadowhawk, p. 124

Mayfly Larva
p. 125

Damselfly Larva
p. 126

Dragonfly Larva
p. 127

Salmonfly Larva
p. 128

Water Tiger
p. 129

Caddisfly Larvae
p. 130

Golden Mayfly
p. 131

Eastern Kayak Pond
Skater, p. 132

**AQUATIC ADULTS**

Giant Water Bug
p. 133

Water Boatman
p. 134

Common
Backswimmer, p. 135

Water Scorpion
p. 136

Mid-sized Diving
Beetle, p. 137

Giant Diving Beetle
p. 138

Whirligig Beetle
p. 139

Water Scavenger
Beetle, p. 140

**NON-INSECT ARTHROPODS**

Sow Bug
p. 141

Garden Centipede
p. 142

Round Millipede
p. 143

Harvestman
p. 144

Wolf Spider
p. 145

Bold Jumper
p. 146

Northern Black
Widow, p. 147

Shamrock Orb
Weaver, p. 148

Yellow Garden
Spider, p. 149

Arrow-shaped
Micrathena, p. 150

Six-spotted Fishing
Spider, p. 151

Flower Crab Spider
p. 152

# INTRODUCTION

THIS BOOK is for bugsters. If you haven't heard that term before, don't feel left out—I think I invented it with the help of my friends. We needed a word for people who are fascinated by insects and enjoy them for no other reason than their intrinsic niftiness. "Amateur entomologist" seemed too stuffy, as did "insect enthusiast" and "entomophile." "Bugger" is out of the question. So are "bug-nut" and "bug-lover," mostly because they sound too silly. I did find the term "entomaniac" popular among some of the people I know, but it probably isn't the best one to use as a recruiting tool. Maniacs are crazy, but we bugsters are merely enthusiastic.

Even the word "bug" is fraught with problems. In the strict language of entomology, a bug is a member of the Order Hemiptera, often pedantically called "true bugs," though I prefer the more neutral "sucking bugs" myself. This latter term refers to the sucking, rather than chewing, mouthparts of this group of creatures. All other insects, including true bugs, are simply "insects." In technical language, when one expands the scope to include spiders, centipedes and millipedes, one has to resort to the phrase "terrestrial arthropods." It's tough to say that without sounding pretentious.

Let's just cut through all of this confusion and call the critters "bugs," and the people who love them "bugsters." These terms work for me, and the only reason they were difficult to arrive at is that our language simply hasn't been called upon to develop everyday words to go with these ideas.

This shortcoming is odd, given the enduring appeal of bugs. Some, like butterflies, are beautiful. Others, like bumblebees and ladybugs, are familiar personalities in the garden. Then there are those bugs that are fascinating in a scary sort of way, such as spiders. On top of all this, there is the wonderful diversity of insect life, and the delight that is generated by such a wide variety of living forms "right under our noses." Biologists these days like to call this wide variety "biodiversity," and some people claim

that we are naturally predisposed to appreciate and crave contact with it. This idea, in turn, is called "biophilia," which can be translated as "the love of living things." I am not sure I agree with the biophilia hypothesis, because there are so many people out there who couldn't care less about the world of plants and animals. For those people who feel the connection, however, the idea of "biophilia" can be a great comfort—it makes us feel normal after all.

Of course, because not all bugs are beneficial to people, and because every single one of them is smaller than a hamster, our society as a whole has developed a rather disdainful attitude toward bugs. As a consequence, most of the people who have acted to improve our understanding and appreciation of bugs have been professional biologists. Of these scientists, entomologists study insects, while arachnologists study arachnids. People who study other sorts of bugs are generally called "invertebrate zoologists," and this term can also be used to refer to the whole gang at once.

In Ontario, as in other parts of North America, the tradition of bug study has gone on primarily in the universities, as well as in research facilities operated by various levels of government. Forest and crop pests have attracted their share of attention, as have biting flies and other bugs of medical or veterinary importance. Ontario has been especially blessed with both the presence of the Canadian National Collection of Insects in Ottawa, and the large number of insect systematists working for Agriculture and Agrifood Canada. There have also been many talented and devoted amateurs who have contributed to the knowledge of Ontario's bugs.

We are experiencing a resurgence of interest in our arthropod neighbours, what with a proliferation of bug-related movies, children's books and toys in the last few years. I suppose this book will probably be considered part of the same "craze," but I also hope it will survive beyond that. For this reason, I have tried to make the book as entomologically correct as I could muster, while still retaining a spirit of fun and informality. Having actively participated in the dinosaur craze of the 1980s, it seems to me that after the wave (or trend) has passed, it is important to remember that we are still left with an interesting subject. As well, the interesting things about it are still generated by the core group of people who cared about it before the fad, and they will continue to care in the future.

I would guess that there are about 30,000 species of bugs in Ontario. This number is a wild guess, of course, and the reason we don't know exactly is that there are still new species waiting to be discovered by science, and there are many species known elsewhere that are waiting to be found here in Ontario. Choosing the 125 "coolest" species was a challenge for me. I tried to pick bugs that are either

**1) big,**

**2) colourful,**

**3) really hard to miss, or**

**4) extremely weird.**

The point of this book is to introduce you to the bugs of Ontario, not to serve as a guide to the whole kit and caboodle (whatever a "caboodle" might be). I hope you realize that to a hardcore bugster like myself, every single one of those 30,000 species has the potential to be wonderfully interesting in its own right. In other words, this book is supposed to be inspiring more than scholastic.

Before launching into the bugs themselves, let's take a moment to orient ourselves to the province of Ontario. By Canadian standards, this province is a relatively warm, lush place to live, because much of it lies south of the 49th parallel, the border between most of western Canada and the United States.

*A lake in the Canadian Shield*

Southern Ontario, nestled in the Great Lakes region and extending eastward towards Montreal in Québec, is blessed with the diversity of life that is typical of the so-called eastern deciduous forests. These forests are also called the Carolinian Woodlands in the far south and the Mixed Deciduous Woodlands over the rest of Southern Ontario. This region (where most of the people live as well) is characterized by a high diversity of tree species, which in turn results in a variety of habitat and forest types and plenty of interesting flowers, birds and bugs to go with them.

As one moves northward into Northern Ontario (much of which is still south of the 49th parallel!) the landscape changes, and the Canadian Shield creates a mosaic of lakes, forests and exposed bedrock. The shield country is full of clear lakes and lovely forests, but the dominant tree species are not as diverse as they are down south. In fact, birch, poplar, maple and spruce account for much of the forests in this area.

The portion of Ontario that is geographically north (as opposed to politically north) is for the most part also shield country. Most of Northern Ontario is considered part of the Boreal Forest, which covers about half of Canada, from the MacKenzie River delta in the Northwest Territories to the Maritimes in the east. However, the cooling influence of the James and Hudson bays produces a thin band of Arctic tundra along the northernmost edge of Ontario, and it is an interesting region in its own right. In many ways, the entomological sweep of Ontario surpasses that of any other province, making it a wonderful place to be a bugster, and a fascinating place to explore.

14

# BASIC BUG BANTER

LIKE ANY science, the study of bugs has its own jargon. Some of its words have plain-language equivalents, but others do not. Unavoidably, then, it is important to get the gist of things before going on to read more about the bugs themselves. I suppose I could have presented this section as a glossary, but I think it will be more interesting as a sort of condensed textbook. I hope you agree.

## Bug Structure

Let's start with the structure, or anatomy, of bugs, and let's also start at the front end of an average, full-grown specimen. Bugs all have a **head**, and on the head there are almost always **eyes** (with either one lens or many), a **mouth**, a set of appendages called **mouthparts** and a pair of feelers called **antennae** (singly an **antenna**). Eyes with multiple lenses are called **compound eyes**; eyes with one lens are called **ocelli** (singly an ocellus). A group of mouthparts that form a drinking tube is called a **proboscis**.

On many bugs, the head is joined to the rest of the body by an obvious line or groove, and it is somewhat moveable on a flexible but very short neck. On others (spiders, for example), the head is part and parcel of a larger body part that also bears the legs—**the cephalothorax**. Major body parts, which

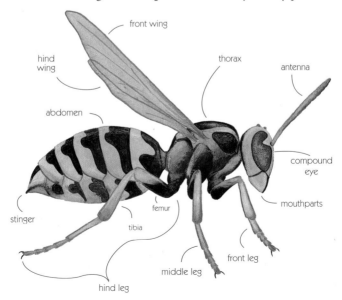

front wing

hind wing

thorax

antenna

abdomen

compound eye

stinger

femur

mouthparts

tibia

front leg

middle leg

hind leg

15

is to say the head, thorax, cephalothorax or abdomen, are often further divided into **segments**, and the segments may or may not be easy to recognize on the surface.

Insects have a separate **thorax**, which is easy to recognize because it is the part of the body that bears the legs. The thorax is, in turn, divided into three segments, each of which bears a single pair of legs. If **wings** are present, the two pairs are borne by the middle and hind segments. In many groups, the front wings are thickened and serve as wing-covers for the hind wings. The three segments that make up the thorax are the **prothorax**, **mesothorax** and **metathorax**. On beetles, the only part of the thorax that is visible from above is the prothorax, the top of which is called the **pronotum**.

Everything past the thorax is called the **abdomen**. At the tip of the abdomen, one finds the **anus**, the **reproductive structures** and, in many types of bugs, a rear-facing set of "feelers" called **cerci** (singly a **cercus**).

There are few other obvious aspects to the anatomy of a bug, but they include **spiracles** on the sides of the thorax and abdomen (openings for the multi-branched breathing tubes of insects, called the **tracheal system**) or **book lung openings** on the undersides of spiders, near the silk-producing **spinnerets**. Some **aquatic** insects (insects that live in the water) have **gills** as well, most of which are leafy or finely branched projections from the body.

## Life History

Now let's discuss life history. Most bugs begin life as an **egg**. The egg then hatches into a baby bug, but not all baby bugs look like their parents. Generally, if the newly hatched young look more or less like the adults (baby grasshoppers, for example), they are likely to be called **nymphs**. If the young are clearly different from the adults, the word **larva** is more widely used (although the larvae of butterflies and moths are called caterpillars). Some

*Larva*          *Pupa*          *Larva*

| | | |
|---|---|---|
| *Pupa* | *Larva (nymph)* | *Larva (naiad)* |

aquatic nymphs are called **naiads**, and spider babies are simply **spiderlings**. Entomologists have recently agreed to use the word "larvae" to refer to all sorts of immature insects, but they have to fight a long history of confusion to do so. If you think this is complicated, compare it to the situation with mammals, where you have to distinguish among pups, kids, calves, kits, foals, colts, lambs and so on.

As bugs grow, they have to shed their outer covering, which is called the **exoskeleton** (or more properly, the **exocuticle**), numerous times. Some bugs simply increase in size until they are large enough and mature enough to reproduce. Others show more obvious changes as they grow, the most noticeable of which is the development of wings and **genitalia** (sexual parts). The genitalia of bugs are often complicated, involving hooks and claspers, as well as things that look like levers, pliers, syringes and the like. Sometimes the genitalia are visible from the outside and sometimes not. In spiders, one pair of mouthparts (the **pedipalps**) serves as the male sex organs, and in dragonflies and damselflies the males have one set of genitalia at the tip of the abdomen and another at the base. The **base** of a structure, by the way, is always the place where it attaches to the rest of the body.

When a bug reaches the full-grown, ready-to-reproduce state, it is simply called an **adult**. However, in order for caterpillars and other grub-like larvae to become adults, they first have to enter into a resting stage, called the **pupa** (the plural is **pupae**), during which the amazing transformation takes place. Butterfly or moth pupae are sometimes called **chrysalides** (singly a **chrysalis**), and remember that the silk covering that some caterpillars make when they pupate, and not the pupa itself, is called a cocoon. Moth caterpillars often make cocoons, while most butterfly caterpillars do not.

The change from young to adult is called **metamorphosis**, and there are three sorts. If the change is gradual, what we have is **gradual metamorphosis**.

If it involves the development of wings, or some other fairly major change in body form (but not a pupa stage), it is called **incomplete metamorphosis**. If it involves a pupa stage, it is called **complete metamorphosis**. These terms are old-fashioned, and, of course, there is nothing defective about an insect with "incomplete" metamorphosis.

# Ecology

The **ecology** of bugs has to do with how they interact with other living things and with their non-living environment. The place where an insect lives is called its **habitat**, a word that means about the same as environment. Collectively, all of the plants and animals in a given habitat are called a **community**, and even larger such groupings are called **ecosystems**. An insect may recognize its habitat by soil type, by slope (or flatness), by altitude, by water characteristics (flow speed, dissolved oxygen, temperature and so on) or by the presence of specific types of prey or species of plants. When insects eat plants, the plants are called **host plants** or **food plants**, and the insects are called **herbivores**. If an insect drinks nectar, the plants are called **nectar plants**. Insects that eat other creatures are **predators**, and the creatures they eat are **prey**. If an insect lives on or inside a host animal, and either kills it very slowly or not at all, it is called a **parasite**. If it is a parasite only in the larval stage, it is called a **parasitoid**. If an insect eats things that are already dead, it is called a **scavenger**. If it eats poop, it is said to be **coprophagous**. Complex, isn't it?

There, that should do it for ecology. Now on to systematics.

# Bug Systematics

**Systematics** is the study of how living things are related, in an **evolutionary** sense. In order to reconstruct the evolutionary tree of life, you really have to start with the basic unit of evolutionary change, the species. A **species** is a group of living things that can interbreed among themselves in nature without **hybridizing** ("crossing") with other species—at least not too much. Species are grouped with other closely related species into **genera**, the singular of which is **genus**. Genera are grouped into **families**, families into **orders**, orders into **classes** and classes into **phyla**, the singular of which is phylum. This system is called the **Linnaean system of classification**. All of the critters in this book belong to one **phylum**, the **Arthropoda** or "joint-legged animals." These creatures are what I call "bugs."

Within the phylum Arthropoda, I have chosen examples from five classes: the crustaceans (Class **Crustacea**), the millipedes (Class **Diplopoda**), the centipedes (Class **Chilopoda**), the arachnids (Class **Arachnida**) and the insects (Class **Insecta**). The arachnids are further divided into two orders in this book: the spiders (Order **Araneae**) and the harvestmen (Order **Opiliones**).

Because of their great diversity, the situation with the insects (Class Insecta) is a bit more complex. Beginning with the flightless insects, entomologists start with springtails (Order **Collembola**). These insects show gradual metamorphosis. After the springtails we come to the insects with wings and incomplete metamorphosis, beginning with the dragonflies and damselflies (Order **Odonata**), the mayflies (Order **Ephemeroptera**) and the stoneflies (Order **Plecoptera**). Next come the grasshoppers, crickets and such (Order **Orthoptera**, the grigs—the only English word for this group of insects—as more and more people are beginning to call them) and the cockroaches (Order **Dictyoptera**). Sucking bugs (the so-called true bugs) also experience incomplete metamorphosis, and they form the Order **Hemiptera**.

The rest of the insects go through complete metamorphosis, which involves a pupa stage. They include the two-winged flies (the "true flies," Order **Diptera**), the wasps, bees and ants (Order **Hymenoptera**), the beetles (Order **Coleoptera**), the caddisflies (Order **Trichoptera**), the lacewings and ant lions (Order **Neuroptera**) and the butterflies and moths (Order **Lepidoptera**).

By the way, "**ptera**" means "wing," Hemiptera means "half-wing," Diptera means "two-wing," Lepidoptera means "scaly-wing" and so on. If you look into the meanings of scientific names, it will help you remember them, but really there is no substitute for simply memorizing the words and getting on with the more interesting aspects of entomology. Note as well that "species" is abbreviated as "**sp.**" (for just one) or "**spp.**" (for more than one).

In most bug books, the various groups are presented in the order that I have just given. The closely related groups are thus placed together, beginning with those that are most **primitive** (in the sense of resembling the long-extinct common ancestor of the entire group) and ending with

*"Eyeball" Orb-weaver*

those that are most **derived** (a term that means they have undergone a great deal of evolutionary change). In this book, however, I have chosen to reverse the order. This arrangement still keeps related species together and gives you all the insight that the traditional order does, but it also allows you to start with butterflies and moths, rather than springtails. My goal is to get you to like these animals, so I have chosen to begin with the niftiest ones. At the end of the insects, however, I have "artificially" grouped a number of un-related aquatic insects together in one section because that is the way many entomologists think of them—as a unit. The non-insect bugs follow the aquatic insects.

# BEING A BUGSTER

THIS BOOK is not about pests and how to kill them. Sure, some of the bugs are harmful, and I don't object to fighting back against them when the need arises, so long as no other species, such as people, are caught in the crossfire. In fact, you'll find that some of my favourite bugs are pests. After all, it is always possible to admire the positive qualities of your enemies, even in the heat of battle.

Most bugs, however, are harmless, and all good bugsters know that they are the very backbone of the ecology of Ontario (and everywhere else), responsible for everything from pollination to decomposition, soil forma-tion, regulation of other bugs and "weeds," food for birds and mammals and much more. Without apology, I think that all bugs are worthy of admiration and respect and at least a passing glance. If you don't understand bugs, you really don't understand the world in which you live.

Bugs are easy to find, at least on warm days during bug season, which means roughly March through October. This long season leaves us with only four months in which bugs are hard to find—pretty darn good in my opin-ion. Of course, May through September is the best time for bugs, during which time they are downright hard to miss.

Bugs live in almost every conceivable habitat, from the alpine tundra on the tops of the highest mountains to the driest prairie sand dune, the insides of caves, the insides of our homes and every place in between. Still, if you want to go out searching for bugs, I suggest looking for them in habitats such as these:

1) under rocks and boards (and remember to put the rocks and boards back once you look),

*The author and his eldest son, bug-watching*

**2)** on plants and especially on flowers and the undersides of leaves,
**3)** around lights at night (but not the yellow, bug-free lights),
**4)** in the water, especially where there are lots of water plants,
**5)** on bare sandy ground, even if it is far from water, and
**6)** at various sorts of "bait."

My favourite bug baits include various mixtures of beer and sugar painted on trees for moths and butterflies, as well as less appealing things, such as dung and carrion. You don't have to feel bad if you choose to ignore the bug-baiting option—after all, many sorts of bait are downright unhygienic. Remember not to touch the bait, and always wash your hands afterward—something my mother used to tell me often when I was a junior bugster.

In general, bugs like warm weather more than cool, and they are easier to find in sunny places than in the shade. They prefer humid days to dry, but they don't do much in the rain. Warm nights will bring out many flying insects, such as moths, but cool ones will not. During a full moon, bugs are less attracted to lights. Wind does not necessarily deter bug activity, but it certainly makes them harder to find and to follow. Daytime bugs get going well after we have had breakfast, and they slow down appreciably by around dinner time.

The easiest way to get a close look at a bug is to catch it, examine it and let it go. Nets are easy to make, and good ones are also inexpensive to buy through mail-order. Small bugs can be placed in clean jars for a brief period,

*A Nikon 5T lens on a pair of binoculars*

and large ones, such as butterflies and dragonflies, can be gently examined while still in the net. Many can be gently handled. This approach, in my opinion, is the best way to study bugs, and it gives a great deal of satisfaction for very little effort. All of the suggestions that follow involve both more work and more of a commitment to mastering unusual techniques.

If you want to watch bugs without disturbing them, you can do it the old-fashioned way, on your elbows with a Sherlock Holmes magnifying glass, or you can try other sorts of optical tools. Close-focusing binoculars are increasingly popular, and my favourite models are produced by Bushnell (the Legends), Basch and Lomb (the Elites) and Eagle Optics (the Platinum Rangers). Close-focusing monoculars are also very useful for bug-watching—they focus even more closely than binoculars, and I recommend them very highly although they are sometimes hard to find. You might also try a pair of compact binoculars, such as the Bushnell Natureview 8 x 30, with a Nikon 5T close-up lens held in front of them (total cost about $200–$250). This way, you get a clear view of the bug, at a distance of about 45 cm, with both eyes at once.

Depending on what sort of bug you choose to watch, you may need to modify your style. When I watch tiger beetles, for example, I find myself crawling around on the sand, continually moving to follow my subjects. On other occasions, I often place a small folding chair in front of a buggy-looking plant and then sit in one place while scanning the flowers, leaves and stems for interesting creatures on which to spy.

Bug watching teaches us a lot. Because the behaviour of many of our local bugs is poorly known, any of us has the ability to make useful observations once we have learned to identify the creatures we are encountering. On the other hand, simply immersing yourself in the lives of insects and other buggy critters is a wonderful way to make a deep and moving connection with the non-human world all around us. You can be as scientific or as recreational as you want.

If you make detailed observations of particular sorts of insect, it is probably a good idea to collect a few "voucher specimens," so other bugsters can confirm your identifications after the fact (for really easy identifications, a close-up photograph will also suffice). When I was young, the only way to approach bug study was to make a collection. Collecting is still allowed almost anywhere except in protected areas, such as national and provincial parks, but it is less popular now than it was a few decades ago.

If you choose to make a collection for educational or scientific reasons, remember to limit your catch, treat every specimen with respect, take the time to label, arrange and store the specimens correctly, and plan to donate them to a university or museum once you are done with them. Instructions for insect collecting are easy to come by, and, for the most part, you will encounter ill-will only when you collect and kill butterflies and moths—most people feel little sympathy for other sorts of bugs.

Increasingly, bugsters are polarizing into collecting and anti-collecting camps. I wish they weren't, but because they are, I want to briefly discuss the matter. Collectors claim

they do not harm bug populations: bugs generally have short generation times and high reproduction rates, and they recover from "harvest" much more easily than vertebrates. Collectors also point out that the identities of pinned specimens can be confirmed, whereas sightings alone are always subject to doubt. Anti-collectors, on the other hand, are reluctant to admit that

collecting is always innocent, because they believe it must be possible for a large enough group of collectors to cause local extinctions of small isolated populations of rare bugs. These are exactly the sorts of bugs that many collectors seek, so this fear could be well-founded if collecting were ever to become truly popular (which in itself seems unlikely). Unfortunately, these isolated populations also become places where anti-collectors and collectors come into uncomfortable proximity with one another, at which point it is very difficult for the watchers to do their thing with collectors chasing the very bugs they want to observe, and vice versa.

When I try my hardest to be rational about this subject, it seems obvious to me that insect collectors are not a big threat to the insects of Ontario. I believe they are inconsequential. Logging, pesticides and habitat destruction are all of much greater concern. It seems to me that the real core of the collector/anti-collector debate has to do with two rather unscientific human motives. First, no one enjoys having their freedom (or the freedom of their favourite bugs) restricted, especially when no laws exist to back the restrictions up. Second, collectors and anti-collectors seem to dislike the sorts of people that the opposing group represents. Looking at these motives, let's admit that it is difficult to sympathize with those who kill the very objects of their passion. At the same time, it is difficult to take a person's scientific motives seriously when they are willfully unsure of the identities of the creatures they are observing and could easily remedy the situation by catching a few. It also seems clear to me that peer pressure has a great deal to do with the attitudes of individual bugsters—in a group of watchers, no one dares bring out a net; among collectors, the binoculars stay in their cases.

As for my personal approach, I usually go out with nothing but binoculars and a camera, content to watch and admire. When I'm doing something scientific, I also take a net. I sometimes collect a specimen or two, but most of the time I use institutional collections for research. I still find many uses for

*Good insect photography equipment is now inexpensive and easy to use.*

pinned insects (for example, when writing this book), but I no longer feel a deep-seated need to possess them for myself. I try to act respectfully toward bugs whenever I can, but I'll admit that it is difficult to avoid inconsistency when swatting mosquitoes or splattering bugs on a windshield one moment, then treating certain bugs like endangered panda bears the next. The way I see it, this sort of "hypocrisy" is inescapable, and one can use it to either justify a callous attitude toward bugs, or accept it and atone by acting kindly toward them whenever possible.

Another fascinating bugster activity is insect rearing, which is much less controversial than collecting or watching—people who rear bugs are more or less forced to treat them with loving care, and they will inevitably acquire a specimen or two through accidental mortality.

Most often, when people want to rear bugs, they start with some caterpillars and wait to see what type of butterfly or moth they will turn into. To rear caterpillars, put them in a well-ventilated cage and provide them with plenty of leaves to eat. Place the cut stems in water with some means of preventing the caterpillars from drowning in the water supply (I place soft foam around the stems). When they are ready, some caterpillars pupate above ground, but for those that dig into the soil, make sure they have some potting soil or peat to dig in when the time comes. If the pupae don't hatch in a couple of weeks, place them in the refrigerator for winter, and mist them with water every few days (refrigerators are terribly dry places). Take them out in spring, and don't be surprised if sometimes you end up with parasitic flies or wasps rather than butterflies or moths. Rearing caterpillars is not easy: as they grow they require more and more fresh food, and their quarters need to be cleaned frequently. If you have a lot of them, they can be almost as much effort as a new puppy!

For other insects, you will have to be more creative with your rearing techniques, but more information on this subject is becoming available all the time. Temperature, humidity, food and light, as well as making things escape-proof, are all subjects you will have to consider carefully with each new species that you try. Another popular thing to do is to set up a pond aquarium, much the same way as setting up a tropical fish tank, but without a heater.

And remember, if your bugs don't look healthy, take them back to where you caught them and let them go.

Of course, you should not forget the potential of bug photography or even bug drawing. These activities require specialized equipment, and a certain amount of practice, but there are plenty of good books on the market that can help you. With more and more sophisticated photo equipment becoming available all the time, professional quality bug photography is now possible with everyday equipment that you buy at an average camera store.

# THE 125 COOLEST
# BUGS
*of*
## ONTARIO

# SILVER-SPOTTED SKIPPER

*Epargyreus clarus*

While skippers are treated separately from the rest of the butterflies in some insect books, they are butterflies nonetheless. A typical skipper has a thicker body, bigger eyes and a more tapered antenna club than most other butterflies. Most skippers are small and orange-brown as well. The thicker body and bigger eyes make the Silver-spotted Skipper our largest skipper; it is also our most spectacular.

Whereas the upper wing surfaces are brown, the underside of the hind wing does indeed sport a silver spot. The wings of the Silver-spotted Skipper are also long, pointed and swept back like a jet fighter's. These wings make for a very agile butterfly in the air, and the chases that take place among male Silver-spotted Skippers are almost unbelievably fast and dramatic. They remind me of the high-speed chases of hummingbirds. Male Silver-spotted Skippers chase after anything that might be a female, including other males and other sorts of butterflies. Typically, the males set up a lookout perch in an area with plenty of nectar flowers and return to the perch after each feeding or chasing episode. The caterpillars feed on pea-family plants.

> **WINGSPAN:** about 45 mm.
> **HABITAT:** gardens and forest edges and clearings.

# BLACK SWALLOWTAIL
*Papilio polyxenes*

The Black Swallowtail should really be called the Mostly Black Swallowtail because it shows a lot of yellow in the wings as well as (especially on males) gorgeous blue patches and an orange eye-like spot near the tail on each hind wing. The Black Swallowtail is a familiar butterfly in parks and gardens, and it is a joy to watch. The females, which are darker than the males, are probably mimics of the Pipevine Swallowtail (*Battus philenor*), a very distasteful butterfly that feeds on poisonous pipevine plants. Black Swallowtail caterpillars, on the other hand, feed on such things as parsley, dill, celery and carrot leaves.

A number of eastern swallowtails are dark with a blue wash on the hind wing, and all of them are probably mimics of the Pipevine. The Black Swallowtail is not closely related to the Pipevine and is, in fact, the common eastern member of the Old World Swallowtail group, which includes a number of west-

> **WINGSPAN:** about 70 mm.
> **HABITAT:** common in gardens and parks.

ern species and the interesting Short-tailed Swallowtail (*P. brevicauda*) of Newfoundland. Almost anywhere you go in North America, you will encounter one or more of the Old World Swallowtails. We are very lucky in Ontario that we do not have to face the identification challenges that make these butterflies a bit confusing elsewhere.

# EASTERN TIGER SWALLOWTAIL
*Papilio glaucus*

Just as leaves appear on the poplar trees in spring, out come tiger swallowtails from their pupae. Over the next few weeks, they mate and lay eggs, from which poplar-feeding caterpillars develop, complete with a fake snake-head emblazoned on their smooth, green bodies. These big, bright butterflies are downright elegant, with soaring wing beats and graceful lines. While they sip at a flower, they flutter their wings and dance on slender, black legs, which is a trait common to all swallowtails. These swallowtails are also some of the few butterflies with attractive bodies, which are streamlined and luxuriantly furred in yellow and black.

Just as the Black Swallowtail (p. 29) is a member of the Old World Swallowtail group, so the Eastern Tiger Swallowtail is the namesake of the Tiger Swallowtail group. In Ontario, the Eastern often flies alongside the very similar but smaller Canadian Tiger Swallowtail (*P. canadensis*). For a long time, they were thought to be part of the same species, and one pioneer entomologist commented that "such dwarfs ... reflect the effects of wintry cold upon the chrysalis."

**WINGSPAN:** about 80 mm.
**HABITAT:** clearings, gardens and parks.

In reality, the Canadian and Eastern tiger swallowtails are best separated by the fact that some (not all) female Eastern Tigers are dark and mimic the Pipevine Swallowtail, while all female Canadian Tigers are mostly yellow, like the males.

# CABBAGE WHITE
*Pieris rapae*

Our least-loved butterfly is another European immigrant, and its caterpillars love nothing better than to drill through defenceless greens in a suburban vegetable garden. Europeans brought the vegetables here from "the Old Country," and they brought this butterfly too. For many people, this butterfly is the most familiar, and it is certainly common in back alleys and other places where native species rarely venture. Up close, it is not a bad-looking creature, with subtle greens and yellows on a background of milky white.

**WINGSPAN:** 50 mm.
**HABITAT:** gardens and agricultural areas.

The white colour was originally intended as a warning to birds that these butterflies taste bad, but because most of our Cabbage Whites grow up in gardens rather than among toxic wild weeds, they actually taste just fine. The similar Mustard White (*P. oleracea*) lives almost exclusively in natural areas and forests, where its caterpillars feed on wild members of the mustard family. Happily, it seems that the Cabbage White and its native relatives stay out of each other's way—the country whites and the city whites, so to speak.

# CLOUDED SULPHUR
*Colias philodice*

Sulphurs are so named because most of them are yellow. For this reason, they may also be responsible for the name "butter-fly." This derivation, of course, should be credited to the sulphurs that live in Europe, most of which are quite similar to our own.

Over most of Ontario, the Clouded Sulphur is by far the most common species, and where the other species occur, identification can be a tricky chore indeed. In fact, some of the sulphurs are probably the toughest butterflies of all to identify correctly. Still, males of most Ontario species have solid, black wing borders on the upper surface, while females have little, yellow spots within the black. Some sulphurs, despite the name, are orange.

Sulphurs are butterflies of open, sunny meadows and fields as well as mountain tops and clearings. They have a direct, powerful style of flight that really doesn't fit into the category of "fluttering." A great place to find Clouded Sulphurs is in an alfalfa field, where they sometimes fly in the thousands. Clouded Sulphurs go through at least two generations during a typical butterfly season. The first to emerge are not the earliest butterflies of spring, but the last survivors are often the latest butterflies in autumn.

**WINGSPAN:** 50 mm.
**HABITAT:** widespread in open areas.

# SPRING AZURE
*Celastrina ladon*

Bluebirds are fine for some, but for those who love the smaller creatures, there is no more uplifting sight than the year's first Spring Azure. Flashing and dodging, close to the ground, this lovely little butterfly is as iridescent as a tropical parrot and as bright as the April skies above. Later in the season, other species of "blues" will appear, with darker blue colours and more crisply marked underwings, but the Spring Azure comes out first, so it is the species we know and love the best.

The Spring Azure is usually the first butterfly of the year to emerge from its pupa. Most of the other spring butterflies, such as Mourning Cloaks (p. 37) and Tortoise-shells (*Nymphalis* spp.), have spent the winter as adult butterflies, tucked away under bark or among dead-fall. By the time late May rolls around, the last of the azures are looking grey and weather-beaten. Most live only a week or two as adults, and their brief lives wreak havoc on their diminutive beauty. It is the males we see most often—they fly whenever the sun is out, searching for females.

> **WINGSPAN:** 25 mm.
> **HABITAT:** widespread in forest clearings.

# GREAT SPANGLED FRITILLARY

*Speyeria cybele*

The Great Spangled is the greatest of the greater fritillaries of Ontario. The greater fritillaries are a group of big, bold, orange-and-black butterflies, with silver spots on the undersides of their hind wings. Butterflies see things differently than people—much of what they see lies in the ultraviolet range—and these spots are bright ultraviolet beacons to other fritillaries. At a distance, fritillaries attract one another with their appearance, but when they get close, they choose to communicate with perfumes instead. Sound familiar?

Fritillary caterpillars, by the way, feed on the leaves of violets, and they only come out at night. In mid-summer, when the air is just filled with fritillaries, but the violets have finished blooming, you wouldn't think there would be enough violet leaves to go around. Farther west, numerous greater fritillaries all look more or less alike. In Ontario, however, the three common species are the Great Spangled, the Atlantis (*S. atlantis*) and the Aphrodite (*S. aphrodite*). The Great Spangled and the Aphrodite both have brown eyes, while the Atlantis has grey eyes. The Great Spangled is always larger and darker than the Aphrodite.

**WINGSPAN:** about 75 mm.
**HABITAT:** open meadows and fields.

# PEARL CRESCENT

*Phyciodes tharos*

Tiny, bright and proud—that's how I think of Pearl Crescents. These are small butterflies, but they fly with the grace and assurance of a majestic Monarch (p. 42). Sometimes, they even glide, which is quite a feat at their size. They like to perch on a sunlit leaf and spread their intricately patterned wings to the sky.

In Southern Ontario, you will find both the Pearl Crescent and the Northern Crescent (*P. cocyta*), but in Northern Ontario only the Northern Crescent occurs. These two butterflies are so similar that the best way to recognize them is by their ranges. The other differences are so subtle that until recently they were thought to be the same species (and they may still *be* the same species). Don't let this uncertainty discourage you from enjoying them, however. In mid-summer, these butterflies are some of the most common in the province, and they are easiest to find where they have shrubs on which to perch. As for telling the Pearl and the Northern from the other species in Ontario—well, that's a whole 'nother story, best left to a different book.

> **WINGSPAN:** about 30 mm.
> **HABITAT:** clearings and shrubby areas.

# QUESTION MARK

*Polygonia interrogationis*

The Question Mark is a sort of anglewing that is related to the Mourning Cloak (p. 37). These are long-lived butterflies that spend winter as adults, and then they emerge from hiding before most other species pop out of their pupae in spring.

The Question Mark is the largest of the anglewings and the most easily recognized, by its silver question-mark-shaped spot on the underside of the hind wing. Other than the spot, the underside of the wings looks just like a crumpled dead leaf or a flake of bark. On the upper wing surfaces, the Question Mark is generally orange and black or brown, and it is interesting that it goes through two generations per year, with different-looking adults in each. The generation that overwinters as butterflies has hind wings that are orange and brown, with pale purplish edges. The generation that emerges during the summer has hind wings that are much darker, almost all black, but the wings still show the purplish edging. These summer adults lay eggs that develop into caterpillars, pupae and then the overwintering generation.

**WINGSPAN:** about 65 mm.
**HABITAT:** forest clearings.

The Question Mark is a butterfly of the southern deciduous forests in Ontario, and it is rarely found in the north, where it is replaced by somewhat smaller, less exotic-looking anglewings.

# MOURNING CLOAK
*Nymphalis antiopa*

The Mourning Cloak is a big, heavy-bodied, spectacular butterfly. You can hope to see one almost any sunny day that the temperature rises above about 10° C, even in winter. The adults emerge in late July, at which point they are at their most magnificent: maroon with yellow trim and blazing blue highlights, with a bark-coloured pattern on the underside. After feeding for a week or so, they usually but not always go into a temporary dormancy, and then emerge to feed again in autumn. When the snow comes, they tuck in under a chunk of bark, a shutter or a fallen log and hibernate. Sometimes they die during hibernation, and you will often find their remains when you clean out the attic or the woodpile.

**WINGSPAN:** 70 mm.
**HABITAT:** widespread in forested areas.

The first warm days of spring bring Mourning Cloaks back out of hiding, and that's when they mate and lay eggs. By the time June rolls around, a few are still on the wing—worn and tattered, with white wing fringes instead of yellow. A Mourning Cloak can live a full year as an adult, which is nearly a year longer than most other butterflies.

# PAINTED LADY
*Vanessa cardui*

A lovely orange, black and white butterfly, swift on the wing and with a love of thistles—that's a Painted Lady. Often, I hear people say that butterflies used to be very common in the good old days, but now they have all but disappeared. Well, in some places, that may be true. Usually, however, these people are recalling a time when Painted Ladies arrived on migration, and that is something that happens only once every 10 or so years.

The populations of these butterflies build up in the southern US over the course of a decade, at which point they swarm up into Canada by the bazillions. No thistle is safe from the egg-laying females, and a northern generation grows up over the summer. These butterflies don't realize that they should return south in autumn. When winter arrives, all of them die, and we have to wait another 10 years to see them again. There are, however, a few of these butterflies around every year, and sometimes the invasion goes on for two or three years at a time.

**WINGSPAN:** about 55 mm.
**HABITAT:** widespread in a variety of open areas.

# RED ADMIRAL
*Vanessa atalanta*

The Red Admiral is a close cousin to the Painted Lady (p. 38). Like the Lady, the Red Admiral is a migratory butterfly, and it is only common some years and rare in others. The caterpillars do not eat thistles; instead, they eat nettles. So, you really have to admire the contribution the Red Admiral makes to our summer environment. I also like the way these butterflies choose a sunlit patch of ground and patrol it at high speed between basking periods on the ground or a tree trunk. They appear to be territorial and vigorously defend their favourite area against intruders, be they other admirals or not.

**WINGSPAN:** 50 mm.
**HABITAT:** widespread in forest clearings, gardens and parks.

Up close, you can see that this butterfly has a thick body, powerful flight muscles and stout, angular wings for rapid, super-controlled flight. When you find one in spring, it is usually quite worn and dull, with wing markings that are closer to pale orange than red. But when the summer generation emerges, the colours are dark and saturated, and the body is clothed in thick, brown hairs.

# WHITE ADMIRAL
*Liminitis arthemis*

When you see the first White Admirals of the season, the school year is about to end. I could hardly wait to get out of the classroom, grab my net and go searching for the big, beautiful admirals that were flapping past the windows during those last painful days of June. Even from my desk, I could recognize them outside—admirals are some of our most distinctive butterflies. A large, black butterfly with a white band through the middle of both sets of wings pretty much has to be an admiral.

A butterfly called the "Red-spotted Purple" is almost identical to the White Admiral, but it lacks the white band. It is yet another mimic of the poisonous Pipevine Swallowtail (*Battus philenor*). Both the Red-spotted Purple and the White Admiral are now considered members of one species, so they have to share a name. Some have suggested the Red-spotted Admiral because the White Admiral has red spots, and the Red-spotted Purple has no white. Perhaps this compromise is for the best. Most people, however, will continue to use the familiar names and ignore the need for taxonomic consistency. The name "admiral," by the way, was originally "admirable," which makes good sense. Too bad it faded from use.

**WINGSPAN:** 70 mm.
**HABITAT:** forest clearings, gardens and parks.

# COMMON WOOD NYMPH
*Cercyonis pegala*

You've probably already seen this butterfly but have given it little thought. Just about any grassy area in July will have at least a few Common Wood Nymphs fluttering around in it, bobbing about near the height of the tallest seedheads. Follow one, and you'll soon give up on getting a better look—these butterflies almost never sit still, and you rarely see them at a flower. Like all other butterflies, however, they have to sleep.

The sun comes up mighty early in July, and the birds come up with it, searching for food among the dew-covered meadows. Wood nymphs, like other butterflies, don't start flying until much later in the morning—sometimes not until 10 a.m. or so—forcing them to spend five or more hours sitting in the open, hoping they don't get eaten. That's why they have a set of fake eyespots on their forewings that can be flashed at a predator if the need arises. Birds are not too bright, and they often fall for the bluff, thinking they have disturbed the slumber of some glassy-eyed reptile. It really is too bad that these butterflies are not more inclined to show off their wings, because the males have a lovely purplish iridescence.

> **WINGSPAN:** about 60 mm.
> **HABITAT:** grassy areas, mostly in the south.

41

# MONARCH
*Danaus plexippus*

The Monarch is our most famous butterfly, and one of our biggest as well. Most people know the story: the Monarch is a migrant, and our Ontario population returns each winter to a few small areas in central Mexico, where they spend the winter alongside the rest of the Monarchs from the eastern portions of North America. A less-known fact is that the Monarchs we see here are the grandchildren of the generation that overwintered in Mexico the year before. No one quite knows how they find their traditional wintering grounds, having never been there, but they do. Sadly, their wintering areas are threatened by development, although they have been given some measure of protection and are a source of both pride and income to the locals west of Mexico City.

Monarch butterflies make this great migration against huge odds, but they are partly protected by their body chemistry. As a caterpillar, each Monarch feeds on the leaves of milkweed plants, and chemicals in the leaves make both the caterpillar and the butterfly distasteful to birds. The distinctive orange and black colours on the Monarch advertise this defence, and another butterfly copies them to help protect itself. This butterfly is, of course, the lovely Viceroy (*Liminitis archippus*). Viceroys are smaller than Monarchs, but where these butterflies occur together, the birds don't seem to notice.

**WINGSPAN:** about 95 mm.
**HABITAT:** fields and meadows where milkweeds grow.

# PURPLISH GHOST MOTH
## *Sthenopis purpuratus*

What a weird moth! With a big, heavy body, a tiny head and huge wings, this moth is actually quite primitive and has few of the characteristics that we associate with more "modern" moth designs. Ghost moths as a group are sometimes also called swifts.

If you find a good area for these creatures, plan to arrive on a warm evening in early summer just after dark. The pupae hatch underground, and the adult moths dig to the surface to expand and harden their wings. Then, when conditions are just right, they take to the air. The males whirr and dance in the fading light in a way that reminded early entomologists of, well, ghosts! Catching a ghost moth under these circumstances is possible, but difficult. Luckily, they are also attracted to bright lights, which is where most people get to know them.

Female ghost moths, by the way, are heavier than males, and they produce unbelievable numbers of tiny, yellowish eggs, which they scatter in flight on the forest floor. It is easy to get a female to lay eggs in a paper bag (any bag, really) but because the lar-

**WINGSPAN:** about 95 mm.
**HABITAT:** forested areas.

vae feed inside rotting wood, they are not popular subjects for rearing. You may also see this moth listed as the Silver-spotted Ghost Moth under the scientific name *Sthenopis argenteomaculatus*, but entomologists now know that both the purple and orange (silver-spotted) forms belong to the same species.

# ROSY MAPLE MOTH
*Dryocampa rubicunda*

The Rosy Maple Moth should be on the Canadian flag, right alongside the leaves that its caterpillars eat. This lovely creature is indeed rosy in colour, and it has some hints of maple syrup on its wings as well. Although it is a modest-sized moth, it belongs to the spectacular giant silkworm moth family, along with such beauties as the Polyphemus (p. 45), the Cecropia (p. 46) and the Luna (p. 47).

Rosy Maple Moths are quite variable, and some have much more pink on them than others, while the ground colour varies from plain white to creamy yellow. As far as I'm concerned, the more pink the better, especially on the legs of these moths! It's really an outrageous-looking creature up close.

**WINGSPAN:** about 45 mm.
**HABITAT:** forests with maples; most common farther south.

In some parts of the US, the caterpillars of this species can be significant pests of maple and oak trees, but to my knowledge it is rarely, if ever, a pest in Ontario. Best to think of Rosy Maple Moths as wonderful side benefits to living in the land of the maple leaf and admire each one as they assemble around the lights in June. On a good morning, they can be as common as any other species on the walls adjacent to a good floodlight in forested country.

# POLYPHEMUS MOTH
*Antheraea polyphemus*

When a Polyphemus Moth comes flapping into the porch light, everyone takes notice. This moth is one of those that many people assume is a butterfly because it is so amazingly beautiful. The antennae tell the real story: fuzzy or thin and pointy antennae all belong to moths; butterflies have slender antennae with thickened tips. The antennae of male moths are not feelers but smellers, and they pick up on the faint aroma of the females' perfume. Following the scent upwind, the males find their mates in the dark.

> **WINGSPAN:** about 110 mm.
> **HABITAT:** forests with birch and dogwood.

When daylight comes, Polyphemus Moths generally roost with their wings above their backs. If a bird tries to peck at them, they suddenly spread the wings to expose the fake eyes on the wings. Most birds are startled by this display, but it doesn't fool all of the predators. Often, all you find of a Polyphemus is a pile of wings on the ground in the morning.

The name "polyphemus" comes from a one-eyed giant in Greek mythology—inappropriately, this moth has four fake eyes and two real ones, for a total of six. Polyphemus caterpillars, by the way, are bright green, are shaped like an extended accordion and feed on such things as birch and dogwood leaves.

# CECROPIA MOTH
*Hyalophora cecropia*

About the same size as a Polyphemus Moth (p. 45), the Cecropia is less common. As such, it generates even more excitement when it is sighted. Along with the Polyphemus, it is a member of the giant silkworm family, a group separate from the commercial silkworms of Asia. At one point, the possibility of using giant silkworms for making silk in North America was explored. It turned out that they wrap too many leaves and messy knots into their cocoons, so the plan failed. Thus, the giant silkworms remain symbols of the wild.

**WINGSPAN:** about 100 mm.
**HABITAT:** forested areas in the south.

In more populated regions, Cecropia Moths are gradually decreasing in numbers. Some entomologists think their decline is the result of habitat destruction and spending their lives flapping around light bulbs instead of mating and laying eggs. Others attribute it to parasites that were introduced to control Gypsy Moths (*Lymantria dispar*).

Adult giant silkworms have no mouths and live off body reserves once they emerge from the pupa. If you find one, and it poops a light brown liquid, don't be alarmed. The liquid is "meconium" and consists of the wastes left over from the transformation from caterpillar to moth.

# LUNA MOTH
*Actias luna*

Some insects almost defy belief. There is beauty in the insect body form, and beauty in the wing patterns of even the brownest of moths, but the sheer elegance of the Luna Moth is astonishing. Of course, it is also possible to explain this moth's beauty in scientific terms. The pale green wings look like leaves when the moth rests among the foliage of a light green birch tree. The tails on the hind wings are like those of swallowtail butterflies, intended as a lure for predators, though it is likely that bats, not birds, are the ones fooled by the Luna. The white fur on the Luna

> **WINGSPAN:** about 95 mm.
> **HABITAT:** deciduous forests in approximately the southern half of the province.

Moth's body keeps in the warmth of its thorax, allowing the flight muscles to function at their optimum temperature, and the furry antennae are used for smell, to bring males and females together in the dark. It's all so logical, and all so beautiful.

Luna Moths do not feed as adults, and if you catch a female at your light, do try at least once to rear her eggs (which she will lay readily in a paper bag). The caterpillars do best on birch, and the pupae, in their cocoons, need a cool period in winter before they will emerge the next spring.

# TWIN-SPOTTED SPHINX
*Smerinthus jamaicensis*

S phinx moths are named for the way their caterpillars adopt a pose something like the famous Sphinx statue of ancient Egypt. Another name for this group is "hawk moths," based on their streamlined form and rapid flight. I prefer "sphinx," because these moths, unlike hawks, are not predators. Most sphinx moths feed on flower nectar, but some, like the Twin-spotted Sphinx, are unable to feed as adults. They have no mouth. In this way, they are like the giant silkworm moths (pp. 45–46). The way they use the eye spots on their wings is also similar.

The Twin-spotted is one of our most common moth species. Along with its near relatives, it rests during the day with its wings held at odd angles, and it turns up the tip of the abdomen (more so in males). These characteristics all work to break up the recognizable outline of the moth, so that birds will mistake it for a bit of bark or dry leaves. Among moths that fly at night, these sorts of camouflage methods are as diverse as the moths themselves.

> **WINGSPAN:** about 60 mm.
> **HABITAT:** deciduous and mixed forested areas.

# BIG POPLAR SPHINX
*Pachysphinx modesta*

A large female Big Poplar Sphinx probably has the heaviest body of any Ontario moth, and this species' caterpillar certainly qualifies as one of our biggest insects overall. The Big Poplar Sphinx is an uncommon find, and even experienced moth devotees are always thrilled when they see one. Big Poplar Sphinxes also have fairly broad wings for a sphinx, patterned in subtle pastel hues, camouflaged on the front wings and smeared with blue and red on the hind wings. The outer border of the front wings has a wavy outline, which undoubtedly helps camouflage these moths during the day. Their eyes are difficult to see,

> **WINGSPAN:** about 110 mm.
> **HABITAT:** forests with poplar trees.

hidden by the furry forehead and shoulders, and the combination of all these features probably gave this bug its scientific name, which is often translated as "modest sphinx." This name brings up an important point: bugs do not seem to possess a self image, or anything we might recognize as an ego. At least, no one has ever produced any evidence to support the notion. Thus, without an ego, I doubt it is possible for any bug to be either modest, conceited or anything in between.

# SNOWBERRY CLEARWING
*Hemaris diffinis*

Another name for this little creature is the "Hummingbird Moth." Sure enough, when one hovers in front of a flower, uncoils its long, beak-like proboscis and shows off its handsome colours, you can't blame some people for thinking they are looking at a bird. In bird field guides, this insect is usually the only one that warrants a picture. One friend of mine tells me that the first time she saw a Snowberry Clearwing, she crept up for a better look and then felt a deep sense of dread—she realized she had no idea what sort of life-form she was looking at.

Of course, there is nothing to fear about Snowberry Clearwings, and, in fact, they are quite delightful. They are members of the sphinx moth family, and they behave like most of their nocturnal cousins. The only things that set them apart from their relatives are the see-through wings and daytime habits. The caterpillars are

**WINGSPAN:** about 40 mm.
**HABITAT:** open areas throughout Ontario.

typical of sphinxes and feed on a variety of forest plants. The adults are on the wing mainly in May. There are three species of very similar clear-winged sphinxes in Ontario, of which the Snowberry Clearwing is the most common.

# APPLE SPHINX
*Sphinx gordius*

As a caterpillar, the Apple Sphinx is indeed an apple-leaf feeder, while the adult moths take nectar from flowers. The Apple Sphinx is neither our largest nor our most colourful sphinx moth, but it is reasonably common, and a bugster is likely to encounter one without too much effort. In fact, although the Apple Sphinx is found througout most of eastern North America, it is most common in the north. Apple trees, by the way, are not a requirement for this species because the caterpillars will also feed on alder leaves, blueberry leaves and even spruce needles. For a caterpillar to have such broad tastes is unusual among moths—most species are biochemically "geared up" to digest only a specific sort of plant.

**WINGSPAN:** about 110 mm.
**HABITAT:** forested areas.

The genus *Sphinx* was the first genus in the sphinx moth family, Sphingidae, to be identified. The genus *Sphinx* is therefore what is called the "type" genus of the family. A number of other similar species in the province of Ontario also belong to the genus *Sphinx*, so be sure to check more detailed references if you want to be certain of your identifications.

51

# WAVED SPHINX
*Ceratomia undulosa*

*U*ndulosa means "waved," and the name of this sphinx moth probably refers to the many wavy markings on the front wings. When a Waved Sphinx perches on a tree trunk, these markings—through camouflage—make it darn near invisible. When it perches on the side of a house or building, however, it sticks out like a beacon. Bugsters soon develop a sensitivity to any triangular mark on a tree or building, and our pulses quicken each time one appears, in the hope that it might be a good sphinx moth.

Somehow, the moths don't seem to notice that they have placed themselves at risk by resting on a contrasting background, which is odd given the studies that have shown how carefully some other moths (such as White Underwings, p. 55) choose the colour of their resting places. Likewise, it is odd that the big green caterpillars of the Waved Sphinx, once they have finished feeding for their larval lives, wander around in broad daylight, on open ground, looking for a place to dig into the soil and become a pupa. If you find one at this stage in its life (and this is the most likely time to find them), don't try to feed it—give it some potting soil or peat to dig in, and let it complete its life cycle.

> **WINGSPAN:** about 90 mm.
> **HABITAT:** forested areas and gardens.

# VIRGINIA CTENUCHA

*Ctenucha virginica*

When most people learn about this moth, their first obstacle is pronouncing the name. I say "ten-OOCH-ah," but I've heard things as outlandish as "coot-ENN-ee-YOU-tchah." This example demonstrates how *not* to coin an English name—simply turning the scientific name inside out doesn't always work.

The Virginia Ctenucha is a member of the tiger moth family. Ctenuchas emerge early in the summer, and if you catch a female and put her in a paper bag, you'll be amazed at how many eggs she can lay. The caterpillars feed on grasses and sedges, while the adults flutter at flowers and sip nectar. They fly by day and are easy to find in open areas and meadows. The black-and-blue coloration of this moth is—you guessed it—another sort of warning to birds that it tastes terrible. Iridescent blue is an uncommon warning colour this far north, but in the Central and South American tropics it as common as yellow, red and black are here. Thus, we have here an exotic moth with an exotic name, perfectly at home in Ontario.

> **WINGSPAN:** about 50 mm.
> **HABITAT:** clearings, parks and gardens.

# GARDEN TIGER MOTH
*Arctia caja*

Tiger moths are not especially big, but they include some of the prettiest moths of all. The Garden Tiger Moth is one of the largest in Ontario. In a good year this species is easy to find. Like many insects, the populations fluctuate greatly from year to year, but it is easily able to bounce back from a bad year or two because the females lay huge numbers of eggs. The most important factor determining how many moths appear in a given year is the number of caterpillars that survive their first few weeks of life.

**WINGSPAN:** about 55 mm.
**HABITAT:** forested areas and suburban areas.

The bright colours of tiger moths are there to warn predators not to eat them—they are filled with bad-tasting chemicals. Of course, their warning colours only work during the day. At night, when the main enemies of tiger moths are bats, they defend themselves in other ways. Some can hear the bats coming, way above the range of human hearing. When they feel threatened, they make their own ultrasonic sounds, to warn the bat that it is about to get a mouthful of bad-tasting tiger moth. Tiger moth caterpillars are generally fuzzy, and the fuzz can cause itchiness and rashes. They even weave these hairs into their cocoons, so that the insect is protected at every stage of its life, both day and night.

# WHITE UNDERWING
*Catocala relicta*

The underwings are moths of late summer. On occasion, you see them by day, but for the most part they are creatures of the early evening, when they search for sap-flows and over-ripe fruit on which to feed. Their coloration is remarkable, with camouflaged front wings and boldly coloured hind wings. At rest, the White Underwing blends perfectly with the bark of the paper birch tree, closing its front wings over the hind ones. If a bird discovers it, the moth spreads its wings and takes advantage of the brief startle effect to allow it a moment in which to escape.

If you want to see one of these moths, here's what to do: mix up a pot of beer, molasses, rum and lots of brown sugar. Warm the pot up to melt the sugar, then let it cool. Go outside and paint the mixture on the rough bark of poplar trees, then wait until after dark. Sneak up carefully with a flashlight, and try not to snap any twigs. The moths have good hearing, and they will sometimes flee at the slightest sound. Of course, after an hour or so of sipping the alcoholic bait, they seem less concerned about people, and more absorbed in their own inebriated thoughts.

> **WINGSPAN:** about 65 mm.
> **HABITAT:** forests, especially with birch trees.

55

# ONCE-MARRIED UNDERWING

*Catocala unijuga*

This species is a more typical underwing, with the hind wings patterned in red and black. The pattern makes underwings easy to recognize as a group, but in Ontario there are almost 40 species, most of which are so similar even the moth experts can't always agree on which is which. In some ways, this difficulty in identification only contributes to the mystique that surrounds this group. Adding to this mystique are a set of strange names that conjure images of bitter male entomologists who had difficulty with the women in their lives. The Once-married Underwing is joined in Ontario by such species as the Mother Underwing, the Charming Underwing and the Forsaken Underwing. Or how about the Widow Underwing, the Girlfriend Underwing, the Sorrowful Underwing, the Betrothed Underwing, the Old Maid Underwing, the Consort Underwing, the Bride Underwing and the Old Wife Underwing? I guess the lesson to learn from these names, to avoid the pain of love lost, is to spend more time with one's partner and less time out prowling in the dark. Unless, of course, you both like underwings, in which case you can enjoy looking for them together. Underwing caterpillars, by the way, are streamlined and camouflaged, and most of them feed on poplars.

> **WINGSPAN:** about 70 mm.
> **HABITAT:** forested areas with poplars.

# SPEAR-MARKED BLACK

*Rheumaptera hastata*

The wings of this familiar moth are patterned in black and white, with a delicately curvaceous outer margin. Its relatively light body struggles to flap the wings, and thus it doesn't whirr in flight like most moths, it flutters. In fact, only three sure signs show that this one is not a butterfly. First, it has thin antennae with no clubs at the tips. Second, it flies by night. Third, it has a habit of crashing into leaves and branches when it flies, rather than deftly avoiding them.

The Spear-marked Black is a member of a large group of equally enchanting moths, the geometers. They are also called "inchworm moths," because their caterpillars perform the familiar inching-along motion when they travel. Their method of locomotion is also responsible for the names "looper" and "spanworm." Many of the geometers are colourful, and some, like the Spear-marked

**WINGSPAN:** about 35 mm.
**HABITAT:** forests.

Black, fly by day. Almost always, when someone comes to me with a "butterfly that isn't in the field guides," it turns out to be a geometer.

# SIX-SPOTTED
# TIGER BEETLE
*Cicindela sexguttata*

Tiger beetles are exciting. They have long legs, large eyes and powerful jaws for killing other bugs, and they run fast. Some, as an added bonus, are brightly coloured. The Six-spotted Tiger Beetle is widespread and common, and it is arguably the most brightly coloured—a brilliant blue green—member of the tiger beetle group in North America.

These beetles live on paths and unpaved roads through forests. They generally like open ground with few plants (they find it easy in such places to spot prey and run it down), but they will often run about on leaves and tree trunks as well. It's a shame more people don't get a chance to see tiger beetles, but the beetles usually see us first. They are quick to take wing, although they usually don't fly far. It's fairly easy to watch where they land, and sneak up for a good look.

**LENGTH:** about 12 mm.
**HABITAT:** paths in deciduous forests, lawns and parks.

If you watch a tiger beetle, you'll see it chase down food, zip out after potential mates and attack any small piece of debris that might be an edible bug. This beetle only comes out on sunny days, mind you, so don't go looking for it in the rain—that's the time to stick to water beetles.

# CATERPILLAR HUNTER
*Calosoma scrutator*

The Caterpillar Hunter is a ground beetle, one of the biggest and most spectacular members of the ground beetle family. This beetle really does hunt caterpillars, and despite being a "ground" beetle, it spends much of its time up in trees looking for caterpillars to eat. You might think that smooth, green caterpillars would be its favourite, but even fuzzy tent caterpillars are to its liking. With mighty jaws and a head as hard as a chokecherry pit, the Caterpillar Hunter chews through caterpillars' hairy defences and gobbles up the soft insides. In forests watch also for the slightly smaller, and much darker, Frostbitten Hunter (*C. frigidum*) and Fiery Hunter (*C. calidum*). These beetles are black and have rows of red or green, jewel-like pits on their wing-covers.

**LENGTH:** about 30 mm.
**HABITAT:** forests, parks and gardens.

Together, these beetles constitute one of the many factors that prevent the caterpillars of the world from eating the trees of the world. I don't like to think of this service as the only purpose these beetles have on earth, but it does seem to endear them to many who might not otherwise value such big, bold beetles in their midst.

# PURPLE-RIMMED CARABUS

*Carabus nemoralis*

H ave you ever sat in your garden on a warm spring evening and wondered what sorts of creatures are rustling around in the dry leaves? Whenever I hear these rustling noises, it turns out to be the Purple-rimmed Carabus.

These beetles are big and black, with a lovely bit of iridescent purple or blue trim around the edges of their bodies. They come out mainly at night, and they eat other insects, slugs and worms. Thus, they are generally a good thing to have in your yard. When early shipments of ore, from North America to Europe, reached their destination, the sailors would fill the hold with dirt from European shores. In the dirt were beetles, and many of these stowaways have become common in Canada and the US, after arriving in these "ballast piles" of foreign soil.

**LENGTH:** 22 mm.
**HABITAT:** parks and gardens.

The Purple-rimmed Carabus is remarkably well suited to life in the city and is not found in natural areas. Apparently, our suburban gardens remind it of home. Pick one up, and it will release a scent something like rotten fruit. Be careful of its jaws! This beetle doesn't bite unless provoked, but it has the jaws of a predator, and it will pinch you if you pinch it.

# AMERICAN HEMISPHERICAL SAVAGE BEETLE

*Omophron americanum*

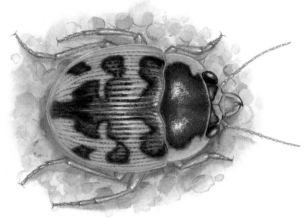

The name alone makes this beetle great—who could ignore a creature that is both hemispherical and savage? Well, the truth is that few people get a chance to see this species, even though it is extremely common in the right places.

To find these beetles, here's what you do: first, find a beach or a sandy or muddy riverbank; then, visit this area at night, with a flashlight, sometime in the summer. Near the water, you should find plenty of hemispherical savage beetles, and American Hemispherical Savage Beetles should be the most common of the lot. These beetles have more green on the pronotum than the other common species, *O. tessellatum*. Both of them look like a cross between a ladybug and a gremlin. Watch a few for a while, and you'll see that they are not only savage (they eat other small insects) but fast, too. The long running legs on these bee-

**LENGTH:** 6 mm.
**HABITAT:** beaches and riverbanks.

tles can propel them across the sand at an amazing pace. I like to keep a few in a terrarium during the summer, on the bedside table. I turn on a seven-watt red lightbulb above the tank once it is dark. Then, the beetles start running around, tussling with each other, digging burrows and hunting. The only regret I have about hemispherical savage beetles is that their beautiful shining colours are almost never seen in the daytime.

# BURYING BEETLE

*Nicrophorus* spp.

Somebody has to deal with them, and you know exactly what I am talking about. Yes, I'm referring to dead mice. Without nature's help, the world would be knee deep in them. That is where the beautiful, orange and black Burying Beetles fit into the grand scheme of things. Flying low over the ground, just before sundown, they spread their many-leaved antennae to the wind, and sniff. They seek the unmistakable aroma of today's death. If they find a big carcass, such as a deer or a coyote, they join their disgusting buddies for a quick snack. On the other hand, if they find a dead mouse, or some other tiny corpse, they rejoice. A Burying Beetle's dream is to find a dead mouse, and a husband or wife, all in the same evening. Then, the couple can bury the treasure, kill the maggots that might steal some of the meal and push the cadaver into a ball. Next, they lay their own eggs and start a family. The Burying Beetle grubs raise their tiny little heads to beg for food, and in response Mom and Dad give them bits of putrescence to eat. Now isn't that nice? Who said that beetles don't possess the ability to show complex behaviour and tender parental care?

**LENGTH:** 15–20 mm.
**HABITAT:** widespread.

# HAIRY ROVE BEETLE
### *Creophilus maxillosus*

To most people, a rove beetle doesn't look much like a beetle at all. It is a long, slender insect, and its wing-covers are short. But a beetle it is, and a good one at that. Beneath those wing-covers are full-sized wings, folded so intricately that you'd swear they couldn't fit.

The Hairy Rove Beetle is another one of those bugs that is attracted to death. Any carcass will do, and it is one of the first creatures to arrive after decomposition has set in. The Hairy Rove Beetle is not there to eat the meat, mind you. Instead, it is there to ambush the unwary. After all, a dead animal is a magnet for bugs. The Hairy Rove Beetle prowls the cadaver and dines on flies, maggots and various other beetles.

**LENGTH**: up to 20 mm.
**HABITAT**: widespread.

There is another whopper in these parts, called the Pie-Killer (*Ontholestes cingulatus*). It prefers to do its fly hunting on top of cow "pies." When it feels threatened, it curls its long abdomen up over its back and exposes yellow bands between the segments, making it look frighteningly like a yellow jacket wasp.

# PINCHING BEETLE

*Lucanus capreolus*

Pinching Beetles are stag beetles, and stag beetles are great. Although we also have some small stag beetles that look a lot like "normal" beetles, the big ones are sure-fire attention getters. Males of the larger species, including the Pinching Beetle, have huge jaws that they use to fight with each other when competing for mates. The females' jaws are much smaller.

The name *capreolus* refers to the Roe Deer of Europe, and, in fact, many stag beetle species are named for their resemblance to members of the deer family. Our largest stag beetle, and our rarest, is the Elephant Stag Beetle, *L. elaphus*. It looks a lot like the Giant Stag Beetle of Europe, *L. cervus*. I think it is interesting that *Cervus* is the genus name for a number of deer species, while *elaphus* is the specific name for the American elk (*Cervus elaphus*). In other words, the name has nothing to do with elephants.

**LENGTH:** about 30 mm.
**HABITAT:** forested areas.

Stag beetle grubs live in rotten wood, and they are actually quite easy to rear in captivity. For this reason, and because they are so terribly nifty looking, stag beetles are extremely popular as pets in Japan. In some places you can even buy them alive from vending machines—something that Canadian society is apparently not ready for yet.

# BESS BEETLE
*Odontotaenius disjunctus*

S tag beetles were once considered a subfamily of the scarab beetle family, and so were Bess Beetles and their close relatives. Bess Beetles and stag beetles share their book-like antenna design with the scarabs, but past that the resemblance begins to fade. Like stag beetles, Bess Beetles develop as larvae in decomposing wood, but Bess Beetles differ in that the adults like to stay in the wood, whereas most scarab adults do not. You can often find large numbers of both adults and larvae in old wood, noisily producing chirping sounds.

Some people call the Bess Beetle the "Patent Leather Beetle" because it has such a hard, shiny, black body. For many a kid who finds a Bess Beetle, the narrow part of the body between the prothorax and the wing-covers is a great place to attach a piece of thread that is tied to a toy car or truck. It is an exciting demonstration of just how strong an insect can be. It is common to hear people

**LENGTH:** about 30 mm.
**HABITAT:** decaying logs.

say things like "If that beetle were as big as a person, it could pull a real truck, too," but the biomechanics of this phenomenon are not as simple as they seem. A person the size of a beetle could probably pull a toy truck, but a beetle the size of a person would collapse under its own weight and have tremendous trouble breathing without the benefit of lungs.

# SPOTTED GRAPE BEETLE
*Pelidnota punctata*

T he Spotted Grape Beetle is a member of the great and famous scarab beetle family. It is not, however, a dung-feeding scarab. Like most members of the scarab group, it feeds on things other than poop. Spotted Grape Beetles develop as larvae underground, feeding on decaying wood, especially on oak and hickory. The adult beetles, unlike some of the larger scarabs, need to feed once they emerge, and their favourite food is leaves.

**LENGTH:** 20–25 mm.
**HABITAT:** forests, vineyards and at lights in a variety of places.

Because they like grape leaves, they are a pest, at least in some places. Like many other pests, however, they do give something back to humanity, and many a child (or entomologist, for that matter) has been delighted to capture a Spotted Grape Beetle and marvel at its elegant shape and movements. These beetles come readily to lights at night, which is one of the most common places to encounter them if you do not grow grapes yourself. For many of us, a beetle that is large enough to examine in detail without a magnifying glass is a wonderful thing indeed.

# HERMIT BEETLE
*Osmoderma* spp.

Hermit Beetles are scarab beetles as well. Like the Spotted Grape Beetle, their larvae feed on decaying wood. The adults, however, are quite unlike the Spotted Grape Beetle, except for their characteristic book-like antennae. The antennae unfold on the end of a short set of segments to reveal a number of "pages" that increase the surface area of each antenna and make it more efficient as an organ for smelling.

The thing I like most about Hermit Beetles is that they remind me of the largest beetles in the world, the Goliath Beetles (*Goliathus* spp.) of Africa. Well, actually, they remind me of the females of the largest beetles in the world, even though it is the males that achieve a record-breaking size. The overall shape of a female Goliath Beetle, with its flattened wing-covers, is so similar to that of a Hermit Beetle that I, for one, feel a deep connection to the forests of equatorial Africa each time I encounter one. In truth, however, these two sorts of beetles are placed in separate subfamilies within the scarabs. Their resemblance hearkens back to a long-extinct ancestor that probably looked a lot more like a Hermit Beetle than it did like a Goliath. In Europe, by the way, a related species of Hermit Beetle (*O. eremita*) is apparently in danger of extinction.

**LENGTH:** 25–30 mm.
**HABITAT:** decaying logs.

# GOLD-DUST BUPRESTID
*Buprestis confluenta*

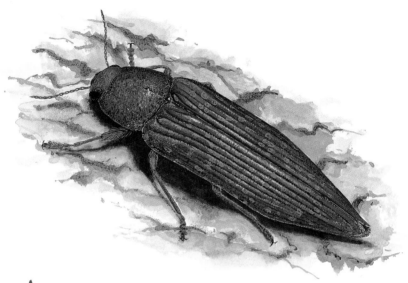

Among those who love beetles, another famous family is the metallic wood-borers. Scientists call them buprestids, and they are also known as jewel beetles. Many of these insects are large, iridescent and almost robotic in their movements. They thrive in the heat of summer, and the best place to find them is on the sunlit sides of trees, where they meet their mates and lay the eggs that will become their "flathead borer" larvae.

One of the finest metallic wood-borers in Ontario is the Gold-dust Buprestid. It is widespread, and its larvae live inside dead or dying poplar trees. The adult beetle is a lovely iridescent green, with flecks of yellow gold on the wing-covers. Once you learn where to look for them, you'll find buprestids in most places that have trees (and even some that don't).

**LENGTH:** 17 mm.
**HABITAT:** forests with poplar trees.

The colours of the Gold-dust Buprestid are unmatched by any other Ontario species, but some tropical members of this worldwide family make ours look puny by comparison. In Southeast Asia, many of the most colourful buprestids are often made into real jewellery. They are set in gold, with their legs removed, and sold for a high price.

# EYED CLICK BEETLE

*Alaus oculatus*

T he largest member of the click beetle family in Ontario is instantly recognizable not only by its size, but also by the two eyespots on its pronotum. Because the Eyed Click Beetle lives mostly in rotten wood and under bark, the eyes probably serve to startle predators that uncover the beetles while searching in these places.

The click beetle family is diverse, and most of it members are confusingly similar in a generally brown and featureless way. Still, they all share the amazing characteristic that gives the family its name—the "click." Turn one over on its back, and it will flail with its legs for a moment or two. Then, it arches its body, and suddenly ... PUNG ... it flips end over end into the air and, like a tossed coin, lands back on its feet roughly half the time.

**LENGTH:** about 30 mm.
**HABITAT:** forests.

In nature, it is doubtful that these beetles fall on their backs on a perfectly flat surface very often. Instead, the click probably functions to startle predators, and some types of click beetles can use the click to launch themselves into the air even before they are upside-down.

# WOODS FIREFLY

*Photurus pennsylvanicus*

Fireflies are really beetles, but that's just another thing that makes them super interesting. The "light" on a firefly is easy to see as a yellowish patch on the end of the abdomen. These beetles flash their living lights at night as a means of finding and courting potential mates. The light is produced by a chemical reaction that is reversible and under the control of the firefly's brain. As such, it is not hot, nor does it "burn out." Firefly researchers have found that a tiny light-emitting diode on the end of a fishing rod, attached to a battery and a switch, can be made to imitate a real firefly, and much of firefly behaviour has been studied with this technique.

**LENGTH:** about 12 mm.
**HABITAT:** deciduous forests.

Firefly larvae also glow, and they are known as glow worms. A variety of other beetles can also produce light, and although we don't have any here, there are many glowing beetles in warmer parts of the world that are easy to confuse with the true fireflies.

I often hear people say that fireflies are much less common now than they were in the recent past, and in places where good firefly habitat has been destroyed (woodlands and wet meadows especially), I believe them. For most of us, however, the sad truth is that the older we get the less time we spend on romantic walks in the dark, and the less often we see things like fireflies, shooting stars and northern lights.

# GOLDENROD SOLDIER BEETLE

*Chauliognathus pensylvanicus*

While most beetles have hard, thick wing-covers, soldier beetles have wing-covers that are thin and flexible. Some look a lot like fireflies, but the head of a firefly is almost always hidden, while that of a soldier beetle is easy to see.

The Goldenrod Soldier Beetle is probably our most commonly encountered species, and it spends most of its time in flowerheads, feeding on nectar and on other insects, in plain view of a variety of potential enemies. It stands to reason that these habits mean it is protected from predators, and its yellow-and-black colour pattern is evidence of this as well. In fact, soldier beetles possess a defence chemical, called cantharidin, that gives their family its technical name, the Cantharidae. This chemical is the same one that allows blister beetles to cause blisters on human skin, and it is very effective at discouraging birds from eating beetles that contain it. Oddly, however, toads seem immune to the effects of cantharidin, and they sometimes eat large numbers of blister and soldier beetles without suffering ill effects.

> **LENGTH:** about 12 mm.
> **HABITAT:** on flowers, especially goldenrod.

# RED FLAT BARK BEETLE

*Cucujus clavipes*

Split enough firewood, and eventually you will find a Red Flat Bark Beetle. They don't live right inside the wood; they live under the bark of rotting trees. That, of course, is why they are so flat—there isn't much room between the bark and the wood of your average stump, and the Red Flat Bark Beetle doesn't want to work any harder than necessary to get around. The larvae of Red Flat Bark Beetles also live under bark, and they too are flattened. This niche is not a particularly safe place to hang out, mind you. The scratchings of a beetle under the bark can alert woodpeckers that something edible is only a few well-placed beak chops away.

The jaws of both the larvae and the adults face forward and have a distinctly fierce look to them, which is appropriate for bugs that eat other insects. They get inside the tunnels of such forest pests as bark beetles (family Scolytidae) and the larvae of various long-horned beetles and jewel beetles. Then they hunt the tunnellers down and devour them. If Red Flat Bark Beetles were more common, they could do more good for forestry. Alas, they are not, and it is always a pleasure to find one.

**LENGTH:** about 12 mm.
**HABITAT:** under bark on decaying trees.

# MULTICOLOURED ASIAN LADYBUG

*Harmonia axyridis*

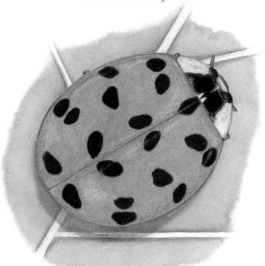

Ladybugs eat aphids, and because aphids eat crops and garden plants, ladybugs are generally considered good. Back in the 1920s, entomologists figured that more kinds of ladybugs would mean more goodness, so they brought the Multicoloured Asian Ladybug over from Asia and released hundreds of them in Washington State, Delaware and Georgia. The Multicoloured Asian Ladybug is now the most common species on both the east and west coasts, and it is rapidly colonizing the centre of the continent as well. In some places, it has become notorious for its habit of invading buildings by the hundreds

**LENGTH:** 5 mm.
**HABITAT:** widespread.

of thousands in preparation for winter hibernation. Somehow, no one anticipated this habit when the species was imported to North America.

To those of us who care about our native ladybugs, the Multicoloured is now the bad guy, because it displaces its native relatives. It's hard to be too angry with them, mind you. After all, they are still ladybugs, and among beetles the ladybugs are almost everyone's favourites. It's just too bad we think of them as little employees, sent out into the fields to do a job for us by killing our pests. Like us, they are just trying to make a living.

# NOTABLE SAWYER

*Monochamus notatus*

Everyone who loves beetles dreams of the tropics. There, most of the beetles are much like our own, except that the biggest ones are much, much bigger. It is a thrill, then, to find a beetle in your own backyard that is a miniature replica of the great *Batocera* longhorn beetles of Asia and Australia. The Notable Sawyer has an exotic look, with its grey, mottled body, elegant shape and long, curved antennae. The male's antennae are longer than the female's, but the female is a bigger beetle overall.

**LENGTH:** up to 35 mm, not including antennae.
**HABITAT:** forests with spruce.

These marvellous creatures emerge in mid-summer, from pupae that are formed just below the bark, inside dead pine and spruce trees. The larvae excavate long, winding galleries through the wood, and somehow the adults chew their way out of the wood without harming their long antennae or slender legs.

When Notable Sawyers take flight to find a mate, they are noisy and awkward, flying with their legs splayed out to the sides and their bodies held straight up and down. When one accidentally crashes into a car or a person, the forests predictably ring with the cry: "What the HECK is THAT!?" A smaller, darker relative—the Spruce Sawyer (*M. scutellatus*)—is also common in Ontario.

# LOCUST BORER
*Megacylenne robiniae*

This longhorn beetle doesn't have as many famous tropical relatives as the sawyers. The longhorn beetles are a very diverse family, and entomologists have divided the family into subfamilies to make sense of their diversity. Hard-core bugsters learn to recognize the subfamilies of longhorns, along with the subfamilies of scarab beetles and ground beetles.

The Spruce Sawyer (*Monochamus scutellatus*) is a lamiine ("LAM-ee-ine"), and the Locust Borer is a cerambycine ("serr-am-BISS-ine"). Many cerambycines have colourful wing-covers, and the Locust Borer is one of the nicest. Bugsters sometimes call the whole family "bissids," an abbreviation of the technical term cerambycid ("serr-am-BISS-id").

The larvae of the Locust Borer are wood-borers, and the black locust tree is their favourite host. Where this tree is native in the US, the beetle is considered a forest enemy. Where the tree is an introduced species, the beetle is considered a control agent, because black locust trees can invade and damage native ecosys-

> **LENGTH:** 15–20 mm.
> **HABITAT:** common in goldenrod flowers.

tems. Many cerambycines feed at flowers, however, and this one is especially fond of doing so. Look especially on goldenrod flowers in the last days of summer, and look carefully because the beetles look like Yellow Jacket wasps (p. 83) at a distance.

The antennae of male Locust Borers are longer than their bodies, while those of the female are shorter. As usual among beetles, however, the female has a heavier body—she is the one that carries the eggs.

# DOGBANE BEETLE

*Chrysochus auratus*

The Dogbane Beetle is another one of those insects that are so darn pretty you really can't walk past them without a second glance. It looks like a great big, carefully polished, bright, shining, iridescent ladybug—at some angles blue, sometimes green or even yellow and red. Its body is round and plump, and its legs end in pudgy, padded, little paws. In other words, it's a cute beetle, and a gorgeous one as well.

As a member of the leaf beetle family, the Dogbane Beetle, sure enough, eats leaves. In particular, it eats the leaves of dogbanes and milkweeds. These plants produce toxic chemicals to discourage animals from eating them. The beetle also has chemical defences, and it will ooze droplets of distasteful liquid when grasped.

**LENGTH:** 10 mm.
**HABITAT:** on dogbane and sometimes milkweed plants.

The beetle's first line of defence, however, is the same as most other leaf beetles—it tucks its legs in and drops to the ground. The Dogbane Beetle is the eastern equivalent of the Blue Milkweed Beetle (*C. cobaltinus*), and, like its western cousin, it prefers dogbane plants to milkweed.

# BIRD-POOP WEEVIL
*Cryptorhynchus lapathi*

Weevils are beetles, and, in fact, there are more species in the weevil family than in any other beetle family worldwide. Entomologists are fond of telling others that one in four species of animals known to science is a beetle, and one in six is a weevil.

The great success of the weevil family seems to have something to do with the way their heads are constructed. The jaws of weevils are at the end of a long snout, called a rostrum, and they are operated by long, tendon-like rods that attach to muscles in the main part of the head. Weevils use their rostrum both in feeding and as a drill with which they prepare a hole before laying their eggs.

The Bird-poop Weevil has an additional survival trick: it looks for all the world like a small bit of dried-up, black-and-white bird poop, something every bird recognizes and none wants to eat. Among insects, bird-poop mimicry is actu-

**LENGTH:** about 8 mm.
**HABITAT:** open or shrubby areas.

ally quite common. In Ontario, most of the examples are moths, which hide by day in plain sight, looking like an accident on a leaf or a twig.

# PAVEMENT ANT

*Tetramorium caespitum*

Ants are social creatures, and for this reason it is impossible to prevent some people from comparing them to us. In my opinion, to do so is a mistake. For one thing, ant societies are made up almost entirely of females that never reproduce. Imagine that in human terms, and hopefully you'll stop right there. If you need further convincing, picture a society where there is only one mother, and she gives birth dozens of times every day.

**LENGTH:** 3–4 mm.
**HABITAT:** open places, especially around people.

I grew up believing that there are two kinds of ants—red and black—and that they are constantly at "war" with one another. Well, that's baloney. The Pavement Ant is an introduced species that is originally from Europe, and it is neither red nor black (nor is it particularly hostile to other sorts of ants).

Here in Ontario, it does well in open places that are relatively warm, and it commonly makes nests in cracks in pavement or sidewalks. It can be a bit of a pest, but for the most part, it is just one more "weedy" species of animal, like the house sparrow, that is slowly but surely establishing itself all around the world. In Scotland, however, the native colonies of Pavement Ants are considered endangered.

# CARPENTER ANT

*Camponotus* spp.

Carpenter Ants are not termites (and termites are not "white ants"). Carpenter Ants and termites are both social insects, but ants go through a pupal stage as they grow while termites do not. As well, all worker ants are adult females, while worker termites come in all ages and both sexes. Carpenter Ants are the biggest ants in Ontario, and they are also slow moving and not particularly aggressive. They have no sting, and their main defence is to bite. Their jaws are strong because they chew through wood for a living, and that is where they are similar to termites.

In the wild, you can spot a carpenter ant nest in a tree trunk by the pile of sawdust outside the entrance of the tree. Carpenter Ants sometimes build their home inside the woodwork of older houses, and there again the thing to watch for is sawdust. They don't actually eat the wood, but in the course of excavating their gal-

**LENGTH:** 10–15 mm.
**HABITAT:** forests, parks and suburban areas.

leries, they certainly do weaken it, to the point where the tree, or the expensive house, may "fail," as the engineers say. Woodpeckers love to eat these ants, and it is fitting that our biggest ant is continually under attack from our biggest woodpecker, the pileated woodpecker.

# BUMBLEBEE
*Bombus* spp.

Bumblebees have a painful sting, but they are so cute and fuzzy that we love them just the same. They are slow to anger, and quite docile, even when you are near their nest. In spring, queens set up new colonies in the abandoned burrows of mice and voles, as well as other underground shelters. There, they make wax pots, with open tops. Inside these pots, they rear their grubs. Once the grubs grow up to be worker bees, the number of pots increases, and some are used to rear the young while others are filled with pollen or honey.

Bumblebees visit flowers to gather both pollen and nectar. Their wings are so small for the size of their bodies that some biologists were unsure for a while about how they could possibly fly. Because they are so hairy, Bumblebee bodies look bigger than they are. The hair helps hold body heat when they fly, and they can fly at lower temperatures than many other bees. One friend of mine claims that when the Bumblebees come out in spring, so do the bears, and when the bees go in for winter, the bears do, too.

**LENGTH:** about 10–25 mm.
**HABITAT:** widespread.

# PIGEON HORNTAIL

*Tremex columba*

Horntails are our largest sawflies, and sawflies are a group unto themselves, on par with bees, wasps and ants. In general, sawflies are pretty inconspicuous insects, but this one gets its share of attention. The adults are big, heavy-bodied and weird-looking, and the females have a pointed ovipositor that makes them look even more fearsome. Fortunately, the females are not dangerous, and the ovipositor is not a sting. Instead, it is used to drill into the wood of trees, where the female lays her eggs, one at a time.

The larvae of the Pigeon Horntail are wood-borers, and some of the horntails are considered pests in some places. When the Pigeon Horntail bores into lumber, the tunnels of the larvae are conspicuous and difficult to hide. It is a general rule that the larvae of insects that go through a pupa stage are larger and heavier than the adults, because the transformation from one form to the other is accomplished without the intake of any food. Thus, horntail larvae are larger than horntails, just as caterpillars are larger-bodied than the butterflies and moths that they turn into.

**LENGTH:** about 30 mm.
**HABITAT:** forested areas.

81

# BALD-FACED HORNET
*Dolichovespula maculata*

If they didn't sting so much, these would be some of our most watchable bugs. Bald-faced Hornets live in colonies, like Honey Bees (*Apis mellifera*), and they build huge paper nests, usually high in the branches of trees. To make the paper for the nests, they chew on bark or wood, and mix the pulp with saliva. They then add each mouthful to the nest, forming either six-sided cells, where the larvae are reared, or the multi-layered outside cover of the nest. Because each load of pulp comes from a different source, you can see a subtle pattern of grey bands in the paper of the nest. If these hornets are coming to your fence or lawn furniture for pulp, you will soon notice a series of shallow grooves where they have chewed.

By the time late summer rolls around, the nests are as big as basketballs, and the hornets are ready to defend them at the slightest provocation. In autumn, the hornet colony breaks down, and only the new queens survive winter, to start new colonies in spring. The nests don't last long once the leaves fall—birds pick them apart. For food, Bald-faced Hornets visit flowers, catch bugs and are also attracted to fallen fruit and dead meat.

**LENGTH:** about 13 mm.
**HABITAT:** treed areas.

# YELLOW JACKET
*Vespula* spp.

The Yellow Jacket is simply a smaller version of the Bald-faced Hornet (p. 82), with yellow markings instead of white. It's too bad we can't just call them all by the same name; it does confuse people when the names "hornet," "wasp" and "jacket" are used interchangeably. This situation is a good example of the scientific names making more sense than the common names (in scientific terms they are all species of *Vespula*).

Some Yellow Jackets nest in trees, like Bald-faced Hornets, while others make their paper nests in old rodent burrows in the ground. The locations of the nests make them difficult to spot at a distance, and it is always a shock when you are walking through the bush and suddenly dozens of angry Yellow Jackets come swarming out of a hidden opening in the earth. Try not to blame them—they are just protecting their nests. Often, the nests are discovered by black bears, and the bears tolerate hundreds of stings while they dig up the nest and devour everything inside of it. Yellow Jackets, unlike Honey Bees (*Apis mellifera*), can sting repeatedly, although they do eventually run out of venom.

**LENGTH:** about 10–15 mm.
**HABITAT:** widespread.

# MUD DAUBER

*Sceliphron caementarium*

To most people, the Mud Dauber is what a "wasp" should look like: long and slender, with a tiny "waist" and narrow wings. To discover that there are thousands of other insects called wasps, many of which are tiny and compact, and most of which are not even social, is a surprise to most newcomers to entomology.

The Mud Dauber does indeed daub mud to make its nest. Each nest consists of a series of tiny mud tubes, stacked side by each. As a nest is completed, the tubes are closed at the ends. The nest begins to look more like a blob of hardened mud with one open tube attached to one side. Inside each tube within the nest, a little Mud Dauber grub completes its larval life. The adult female Mud Dauber spends her time flying from flower to flower drinking nectar, as well as hunting spiders for her young. The spiders are paralyzed and taken back to the mud nest. Although an entire family of wasps, called spider wasps (Pompilidae), specialize in using spiders as prey, the Mud Dauber is actually a member of the digger wasp family (Sphecidae).

**LENGTH:** 25–30 mm.
**HABITAT:** gardens, parks and near rocky cliffs.

# CICADA KILLER
### *Sphecius speciosus*

M ost wasps are solitary, not colonial. The Cicada Killer is one of these solitary wasps. It is a member of the digger wasp family, and it has fascinating habits.

The females sometimes take nectar from flowers, but for the most part, they spend their days looking for cicadas, those big, noisy sucking bugs that many people call "locusts." With amazing agility, a female stings the cicada in the nerve cord and injects a paralyzing poison. The cicada is then immobilized, but still alive. With immense power and determination, the Cicada Killer carries the cicada back to a burrow that she prepared some time before. She opens the burrow, drags the cicada down into the dark and lays an egg on it. Then she comes back to the surface and closes the entrance. Next, she goes off to look for another cicada, or dig another burrow. Meanwhile, the egg hatches, and the wasp

**LENGTH:** about 30 mm.
**HABITAT:** open areas, especially sandy ones, near forests.

grub devours the body of the zombie cicada. That is, unless some other insect, such as a velvet ant or a parasitic fly, gets its egg into the burrow before it is closed. Then, the invader kills the baby wasp and eats the meal itself.

This wasp, by the way, is not common in Ontario, and it is found only in the south of the province.

# COW KILLER

*Dasymutilla occidentalis*

The Cow Killer is a member of a group of bugs called velvet ants. It is not, however, an ant at all. The familiar wingless, furry Cow Killer is really a female wasp, in the family Mutillidae. The males look more like traditional wasps, and they are smaller and less impressive than the females.

Cow Killers get their name from their sting, and they have some of the most painful stings in the entire insect world. Their bright colours are a warning to potential enemies to avoid them. Cow Killers do not use their stings to kill or paralyze other bugs. Instead, they look for the nests of digging wasps and bees and lay their eggs on the prey that the wasps and bees have gathered.

**LENGTH:** about 20 mm.
**HABITAT:** open areas, especially sandy ones.

Then, the Cow Killer grub eats both the wasp grub and the paralyzed prey intended for the digger wasp. Cow Killers, and velvet ants, in general, are omnivores as adults, and they can live for many months as well. Because Cow Killers are some of the hardiest bugs around, as well as some of the best looking, they are often exhibited in bug zoos, where they make a very interesting display.

# STUMP STABBER

*Megarhyssa* spp.

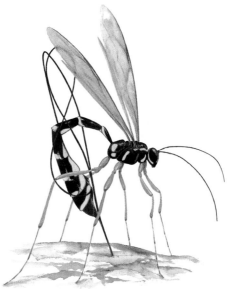

T alk to foresters about bugs, and a few familiar species will come up time and again: jewel beetles, long-horned beetles, horntails and Stump Stabbers, also known as ichneumons.

A big female Stump Stabber can be 85 mm long, including its immense ovipositor, and it looks like something that could definitely hurt you. In fact, many people think the Stump Stabber does sting, despite the assurances of entomologists to the contrary. If you find one, follow it. The Stump Stabber, or ichneumon (pronounced "ick-NEW-monn"), flies from tree trunk to tree trunk, all the while rapidly drumming its antennae while running around on the bark, quite obviously searching for something.

> **LENGTH:** with ovipositor, up to 160 mm.
> **HABITAT:** forested areas with conifers.

Then, she stops. Somehow, she has detected a wood-boring grub, deep in the wood. At this point, she brings her ovipositor to bear, like some sort of strange miniature oil rig. The insect strains to work the tool into the wood, and eventually she finds the larva and forces a slender, very compressible egg down the tube and into the body of her host. There, the egg will hatch, and the ichneumon grub will proceed to devour its victim from the inside out, leaving its essential organs to the last.

# HOVER FLY

*Syrphus* spp.

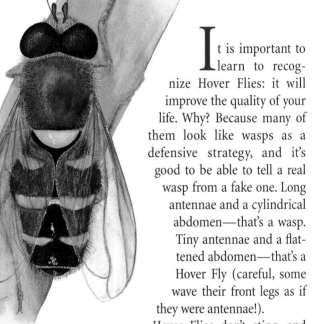

It is important to learn to recognize Hover Flies: it will improve the quality of your life. Why? Because many of them look like wasps as a defensive strategy, and it's good to be able to tell a real wasp from a fake one. Long antennae and a cylindrical abdomen—that's a wasp. Tiny antennae and a flattened abdomen—that's a Hover Fly (careful, some wave their front legs as if they were antennae!).

Hover Flies don't sting, and they don't bite either. They are also much better fliers than wasps. It is important to appreciate how many Hover Flies are involved in the pollination of flowers. They visit blossoms the same way bees do. The larvae of Hover Flies are interesting, too. Some are predators that feed on aphids, while others are the famous "rat-tailed maggots" that live in the muck at the bottom of shallow ponds. In England, many people study Hover Flies as a hobby, and there they enjoy the luxury of being able to buy colour field guides to their local species. Perhaps some day we will reach the same level of sophistication here in Canada, but for the moment just recognizing Hover Flies at all is a good thing.

**LENGTH:** about 10 mm.
**HABITAT:** widespread.

# HORSE FLY

*Hybomitra* spp.

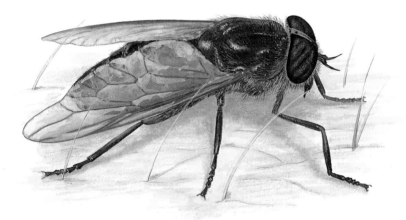

So what could be interesting about a Horse Fly? Well, how about the colours in its eyes? If you get a close-up look at one—perhaps after a lucky swat—check out the eyes with their intense rainbows that enliven their otherwise evil-looking faces.

These flies feed on blood, and they are most common near lakes. Go for a swim in mid-summer, and I guarantee that by the time you have dried yourself off you will have taken at least one swing at a Horse Fly. They are attracted to large mammals (such as ourselves), and the thing they look for is a dark object with a light spot on it, where the sun forms a reflective "highlight." If you drive a black car or a black van, you will find even more of them when you get back to the parking lot.

**LENGTH:** about 15 mm.
**HABITAT:** most abundant near lakes.

One good thing about Horse Flies is that they are so big it's hard for one to bite without you knowing it is there. A smaller version of a Horse Fly, with dark markings on its wings, is called a Deer Fly (*Chrysops* spp.). Given any opportunity, mind you, Horse Flies will bite deer, Deer Flies will bite horses and either one will bite people.

# ROBBER FLY

*Promachus* spp.

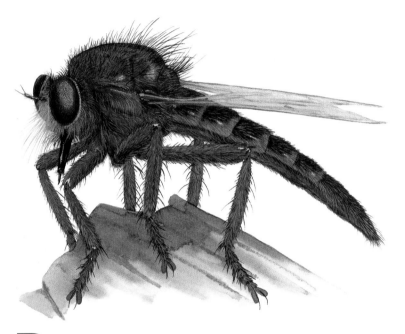

Robber Flies don't really steal things, other than life itself. They are amazingly agile predators, and they kill by catching other insects in mid-air. Between hunts, they find a perch on the ground or on vegetation, and from there they scan for potential victims. With large compound eyes, they have excellent vision and an amazing ability not only to spot their prey, but also to follow it through the air in high-speed pursuit. When they catch something, they return to the ground, with their fearsome proboscis deep in the tissues of their unlucky prey. They are not too distantly related to Horse Flies (p. 89), and they have similar sorts of mouthparts. Even bees can fall prey to Robber Flies, and the flies have perfected the perfect way to kill these dangerous insects, nabbing them in mid-air. Some other members of the *Promachus* group of Robber Flies feed on grigs.

**LENGTH:** about 25 mm.
**HABITAT:** open areas.

# BROWN CRANE FLY
*Nephrotoma ferruginea*

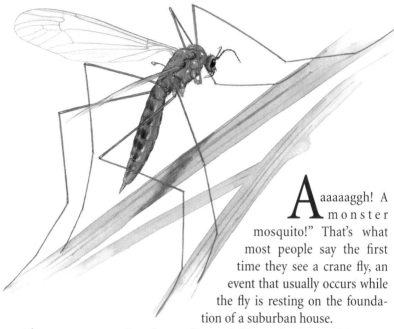

Aaaaaaggh! A monster mosquito!" That's what most people say the first time they see a crane fly, an event that usually occurs while the fly is resting on the foundation of a suburban house.

There are many species of crane flies, and this species is one of the most diverse of all fly families. These crane flies look evil, but the truth is you couldn't ask for a nicer bug. They don't bite at all, they are actually sort of attractive and even the larvae are unobtrusive, living as scavengers in the soil. Some people also

**LENGTH:** about 20 mm.
**HABITAT:** widespread, often in gardens and parks.

call these flies "daddy long-legs," a term that is most often used to refer to Harvestmen (p. 144), which are a sort of arachnid. In general, then, we are surrounded by confusion with respect to crane flies, so hopefully this book will lead the way to dispelling our ignorance. Another frequent twist to the finding-one-in-your-garden story is the fact that they are often discovered while mating, end to end. When a mating pair is disturbed, the sight of two sets of wispy flailing wings, 12 immense dangling legs and two giant "mosquitoes" tugging in opposite directions makes for a spectacle that is, let's just say, "creepy" to all but the most devoted bugsters among us.

# ANTHRAX BEE FLY
*Anthrax analis*

Bee flies look like delta-winged fighter planes, but they are neither fighters nor beeish by nature. You can generally recognize members of this family by their swept-back, dark-coloured wings, and the Anthrax Bee Fly has a distinctive pattern that separates it from the others. Many species have clear wings, and some of these bee flies are easy to confuse with Hover Flies (p. 88).

The larvae of bee flies are parasitic maggots. Some are parasites of tiger beetle larvae, while others live in the burrows of digger bees and wasps, feeding on the bee or wasp larvae or on their paralyzed prey (see pp. 84–85). Because their prey live down holes, adult female bee flies will sometimes flick eggs into the lace holes of your shoes!

Anthrax Bee Flies specialize in tiger beetle larvae, and in some places, a great number of the larvae may be killed. The bee flies are never common enough to threaten the tiger beetle populations, however, and the two seem to coexist after a fashion. As for the genus name *Anthrax*, it probably refers in some sense to coal (as in "anthracite") and has nothing to do with the deadly disease by the same name.

**LENGTH:** about 12 mm.
**RANGE:** throughout Ontario.

# GREEN LACEWING
### *Chrysopa* spp.

Beautiful, smelly and mean—that's how I think of lacewings. They are familiar garden bugs, and the adults are truly elegant with their many-veined wings, their delicate lime green bodies and their bulging golden eyes. The scientific name *Chrysopa* means exactly that: "golden eyes." Catch one, however, and you will soon notice a truly weird smell while it twists and turns in your fingers as you hold it by the wings. The smell is a bit like really bad coffee. As for the mean-spirited aspect of their nature, lacewings are predators, and they mostly eat aphids. Thus, they join ladybugs and the larvae of some Hover Flies (p. 88) in a "friends of the gardener" category, despite the fact that none of them even knows what a gardener is.

Young lacewings, which are larvae much like those of a ladybug, are also aphid eaters. They are so vicious that the mother lacewing lays each egg on the top of a long, slender stalk,

**LENGTH:** about 12 mm.
**HABITAT:** gardens, parks and forested areas.

so the first larva to hatch doesn't eat all of its brothers and sisters before they can get out of the egg. As well as the green ones, watch for brown lacewings and even blotchy ones (both in the family Hemerobiidae), usually early and late in the season.

# DOBSON FLY

*Corydalus cornutus*

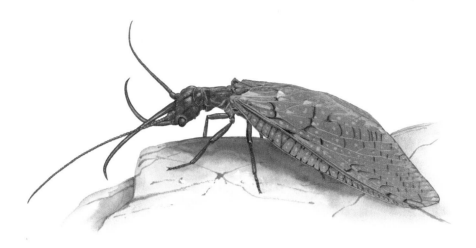

As with stag beetles (p. 64), the jaws of male and female Dobson Flies are amazingly different. The jaws of a female are impressive, but they are relatively small. Those of the male are absolutely huge, extending beyond the head like a pair of gigantic pincers. Apparently, neither sex eats anything once they become adults, and the male jaws are used in courtship and male fighting rather than as weapons to subdue prey (or dig clams or whatever other things you might like to imagine).

Even without the jaws, Dobson Flies would be impressive insects. They are among the largest of the "trout food" insects in this part of the world. The larvae, called "hellgrammites," are also fearsome, big-jawed creatures, and they can give you a painful bite. Fishermen have traditionally used them as bait, however, and it is also common to see imitations of hellgrammites made of fur and feathers by fly fishermen. Personally, I'd rather risk a fish hook in the finger than handle living hellgrammites, but that's just my own style of fishing.

**LENGTH:** 50 mm.
**HABITAT:** near streams and rivers.

# MANTIS FLY
*Mantispa interrupta*

What looks like a praying mantis, acts like a praying mantis, but isn't a praying mantis? Why, a Mantis Fly, of course. This insect is a wonderful example of what is called convergence. In other words, the evolutionary forces that produced one sort of animal (in this instance, the praying mantis) have acted independently on an unrelated animal (in this case, the Mantis Fly) to make them look alike. From the small, triangular head to the grasping front legs to the slender middle and hind legs and to the flying wings folded over the elongate abdomen, you might wonder what separates these two groups. Notice, however, that the wings of a Mantis Fly are clear, while those of a mantis are opaque. Also notice that the front legs attach to the thorax of a Mantis

> **LENGTH:** 20–25 mm.
> **HABITAT:** open areas near forests.

Fly right behind the "chin" of the bug, whereas those of a mantis attach a bit farther back. Then ask yourself if you have ever seen a praying mantis adult (with wings, of course) that is only 25 mm long.

The biggest difference, however, is between the life cycles of Mantis Flies and mantises. Young mantises look like adults, but without wings. Young Mantis Flies, on the other hand, look like some beetle larvae and live as parasites in spider egg sacks before pupating and emerging as adults.

# ANT LION
*Brachynemurus* spp.

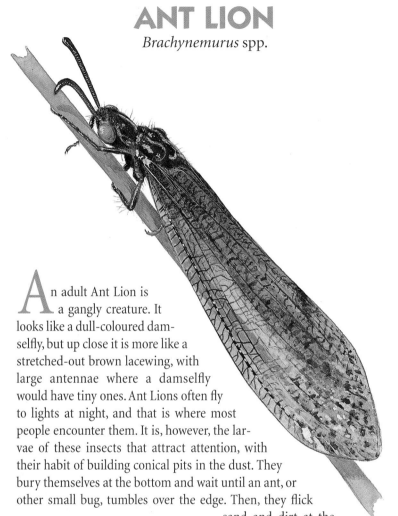

An adult Ant Lion is a gangly creature. It looks like a dull-coloured damselfly, but up close it is more like a stretched-out brown lacewing, with large antennae where a damselfly would have tiny ones. Ant Lions often fly to lights at night, and that is where most people encounter them. It is, however, the larvae of these insects that attract attention, with their habit of building conical pits in the dust. They bury themselves at the bottom and wait until an ant, or other small bug, tumbles over the edge. Then, they flick sand and dirt at the intended prey, which forces it to slip farther down into the pit of despair. When the prey hits the bottom, the larva's jaws close and pierce the cuticle of the victim, sucking it dry through the hollow hypodermic mandibles. This horrific image has certainly been the inspiration for a number of science fiction monsters, and fortunately, it is the sort of thing that only works at the scale of a bug. Larger animals would find the pressures of being buried in sand too much to handle for more than a short period.

**LENGTH:** about 25 mm.
**HABITAT:** warm, dry places with fine sand or silt.

# LEAF-FOOTED BUG

*Leptoglossus* spp.

L eaf-legged Bug" might have been a better name for these insects because it is their legs and not their "feet" that are leaf-like. It is only the hind legs that are flattened and expanded in a leaf-like fashion. Presumably, this colouring helps camouflage Leaf-footed Bugs, although there are some tropical species that have brightly coloured "leaves" warning birds and other predators that they taste bad. The fact that a structure like the hind legs of this insect could evolve for one purpose and then switch over to serve another is just part of what makes the study of insect evolution so fascinating.

**LENGTH:** about 15 mm.
**HABITAT:** on shrubs and low vegetation.

Leaf-footed Bugs feed on plants, especially coniferous tree seeds. They are sometimes pests on coniferous trees, but as pests go, they are not too terribly destructive. Young Leaf-footed Bugs are not as leaf-footed as the adults, and the legs develop their leafiness as the insect grows older.

97

# LARGE MILKWEED BUG

*Oncopeltus fasciatus*

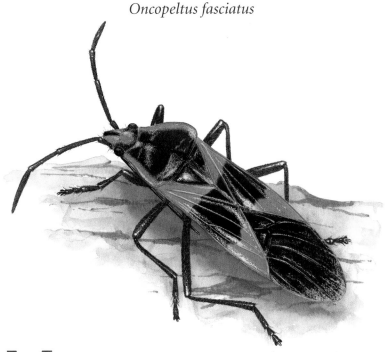

Milkweed bugs are yet another sort of insect that can swallow the poisons in milkweed plants without killing themselves in the process. This ability protects them from a host of predators and also justifies their orange-and-black warning colours. Large Milkweed Bugs feed only on the flowers and seedpods of the milkweed plant. They are therefore found near the tops of the plants, in plain view, where their warning comes in handy.

In truth, this is one gorgeous bug! It is also a popular laboratory animal, oddly enough, and captive colonies will feed on sunflower seeds. They are easy to raise and bright orange-red as babies, with a certain cuteness that defies description in everyday terms (the way one might describe, for example, a human baby, a puppy or a kitten). If a baby bug can be cute, which, of course, it can, then baby Large Milkweed Bugs get my vote for the cutest of the lot. Large Milkweed Bugs, by the way, re-invade Ontario each year. They have difficulty surviving the cold winters here.

**LENGTH:** about 15 mm.
**HABITAT:** on milkweed plants.

# BOXELDER BUG
*Leptocoris trivittata*

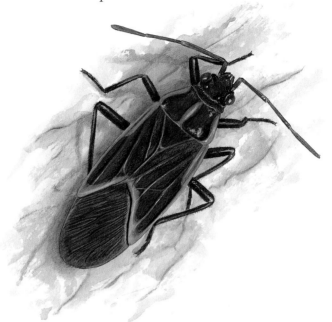

I n some places, this species is called a "Maple Bug," and I know that some people will criticize me for using its official name instead. These bugs feed mainly on the seeds of maple trees and on the Manitoba maple, in particular, which is called the "boxelder" in other parts of the continent.

Boxelder Bugs have a habit of congregating in houses to spend the winter. When the family is gathering around the table for New Year's dinner, and a big clumsy Boxelder Bug goes buzzing across the room, bangs into the chandelier and lands in the mashed potatoes, who can blame anyone for taking offence? It is

LENGTH: about 12 mm.
HABITAT: widespread.

important, at moments like these, to remember that they don't do any harm, and that up close they are actually quite handsome. Bugsters will immediately recognize the function of their black-and-red colours—to warn predators that they taste bad (even though they don't smell bad). When they are young, they are even more colourful, more red than black. It is only when they get their wings, as adults, that the mainly black wings cover the bright red abdomen.

# GREEN STINK BUG
*Acrosternum hilare*

Stink bugs stink, at least they do when they think they are in danger. They do so with scent glands that produce an odour unlike anything else that you or I are likely to ever encounter. This odour makes them easy to recognize up close, but they are also obvious in other ways. Stink bugs have broad, pointed shoulders and a large, triangular plate in the middle of their back (the scutellum, for those who like to know these things). Some stink bugs are more triangular than others, so if in doubt, sniff. Some of them feed on other insects, while others suck the juices from plants and plant seeds. Stink bugs are also known for their great prowess as devoted mothers. A female lays a cluster of intricately sculptured eggs on the surface of a leaf. Then, the mother guards the brood until they hatch, at which point the babies are free to fend for themselves. Baby stink bugs, like all sucking bugs, are much like tiny adults but without wings. The Green Stink Bug is one of our biggest stink bugs and is a lovely green colour.

**LENGTH:** about 15 mm.
**HABITAT:** forest edges.

# HARLEQUIN BUG
*Murgantia histrionicus*

I find animal names amusing. The Harlequin Bug is a type of stink bug with a lovely pattern on its back. "Harlequin" refers to a character in pantomime with a colourful, diamond-patterned costume, vaguely like the pattern on this bug's back. Of course, Harlequin is also a brand of romance novel, which some people find overly dramatic. In a semi-related way, the second part of the scientific name, *histrionicus*, is a reference to over-the-top theatrics. *Murgantia* is more of a mystery to me, but I suspect it means "beautiful mouse." Of course, these names tell us much more about the inner workings of biologists' minds than about the animals themselves. To watch Harlequin Bugs, you'd never think they were theatrical at all. They feed on the juices of plants, especially those plants in the mustard family, and their bright colours are a warning to birds that, like all stink bugs, they stink. Look for Harlequin Bugs in weedy places and vacant lots—they seem to do better there than in natural meadows and shrubbery. Perhaps they have become more abundant with the arrival of "modern" civilization.

**LENGTH:** 10 mm.
**HABITAT:** open places, gardens and parks.

# BUFFALO TREEHOPPER
*Stictocephala* spp.

I t takes a bit of imagination, but if you look closely at this bug you'd have to admit that a Buffalo Treehopper looks a bit like a buffalo. If you think about it even further, you will probably agree with me that the treehopper is by far the more impressive of the two. Treehoppers feed on plant juices, which they suck up with their proboscises.

While these treehoppers are sitting and feeding, they need some protection. Thus, most species have some sort of enlarged, hardened projection from the top of the thorax. In the case of the Buffalo Treehopper, this defensive projection amounts to a hump, with hardened points on its upper corners. Other species have projections that look like rose thorns, and those treehoppers live on (you guessed it!) rose stems. In the tropics, treehoppers really come into their own, with spikes, balls, branches and spines that look more like medieval weapons than parts of living creatures. Treehopper larvae, however, do not possess these outgrowths and remain relatively defenceless.

**LENGTH:** about 8 mm.
**HABITAT:** shrubs and trees.

# CANDY-STRIPE LEAFHOPPER
*Graphocephala coccinea*

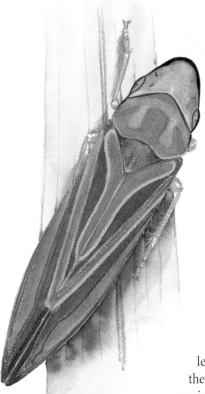

Leafhoppers are related to tree-hoppers (p. 102), and they too suck plant juices to obtain their nutrition. Unlike tree-hoppers, however, they do not develop protuberances on their backs. Most leafhoppers are slim and trim, and most are green or brown. Some leafhoppers, on the other hand, are extremely pretty, and the Candy-stripe Leafhopper is one of the prettiest.

Once you can recognize a leafhopper, you'll start seeing them just about everywhere. Many species are fond of lawns, and it's easy to find these just by lying down on the grass and running your fingers through it. Other leafhoppers are fussier, requiring particular species of plants to eat from. With hundreds of species in Ontario alone, leafhopper identification is a big concern. Correct identification is important for many crop and greenhouse entomologists because many leafhoppers are pests. Many

**LENGTH:** about 8 mm.
**HABITAT:** shrubby areas.

more, however, are not pests, and the Candy-stripe is among the good guys in the leafhopper clan. Nature photographers are especially fond of this little gem. It is one of those incredible discoveries that you can make "right under your own nose" with a macro lens.

# DOG DAY CICADA
### *Tibicen canicularis*

In some parts of North America, cicadas are a big deal, especially when they emerge by the millions, cover the trunks of trees and drown out all other sounds with their incredibly loud buzzing. The larvae of these big insects live for years underground feeding on roots, and they emerge in early summer.

Here in Ontario, however, most people see them much less often than they hear them. To find one, you first have to learn what they sound like—a prolonged whining buzz. That's the male, and he sits on a slender tree branch while singing, often three or more metres above the ground. If you are very stealthy, you may be able to get close enough to spot him. One false move, however, and he will either fly away or shut up. Cicada sounds are produced by a vibrating mechanism in the abdomen, which is made up of a resonating chamber and a thin membrane, something like a banjo skin. For their size, cicadas can be incredibly noisy. By the way, some people say "SICK-uh-DAHH" or "sih-KAH-duh," while others insist on "sick-AY-dah." All are correct, of course, but most entomologists I know say "sick-AY-dah."

**LENGTH:** about 30 mm.
**HABITAT:** treed places.

# EUROPEAN EARWIG

*Forficula auricularia*

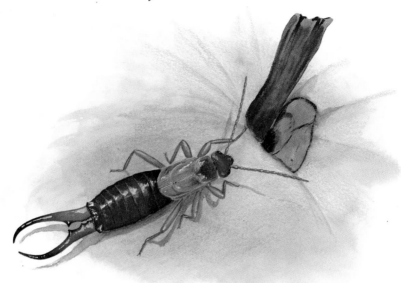

Very few insects generate the confusion that earwigs do. For odd reasons, people often believe that earwigs drill into human ears, that they are filthy and that they can pinch very hard with their cerci. According to entomologists, who should know such things, they don't do any of these things. As for how they got their name, your guess is as good as mine. The European Earwig is an introduced species, originally native to Europe, which arrived in North America around 1919. Thus, the name "earwig" is not of local origin.

Earwigs are interesting, mostly harmless creatures, and they are also good parents who guard their eggs and newborn young. Some are parasitic on other sorts of bugs, while others are omnivores, predators, scavengers or plant feeders. It is the plant-feeding ones that we see most often, including the European Earwig, which is

**LENGTH:** about 12 mm.
**HABITAT:** widespread, including parks and gardens.

actually omnivorous. European Earwigs especially like to feed on flowers, and this flower eating naturally annoys the gardener who grew them. To my way of thinking, however, flowers grow themselves, and a flower with an earwig in it is infinitely more interesting than one without.

# EUROPEAN MANTID
*Mantis religiosa*

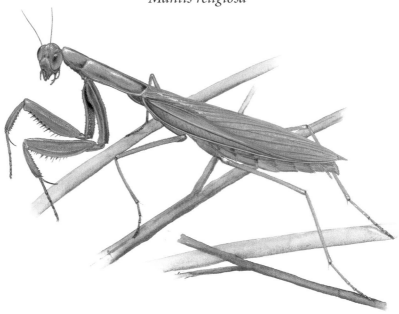

Because mantids can turn their heads and look at whatever interests them, they have a wonderfully humanoid look. Their upright posture and grasping forelegs only add to the effect.

The European Mantid, an introduced species that arrived in Canada in about 1915, is found fairly regularly in Ontario's warmer areas. It is the species that led to the name "praying mantis," inspired by the way it holds its forelegs as if in prayer. The name "mantis" also has a religious meaning: it is a Greek word that refers to prophets. The scientific equivalent, "mantid," is the short form of the family name, Mantidae. Like all members of the group grigs and their relatives, European Mantids are lightning-fast predators, catching other bugs in their spiked forelegs. And yes, on occasion, a female will eat her mate during the act of copulation, and he will indeed continue mating, even without his brain. However, it is a rare occurrence. Apart from this last unfortunate feature, mantids are surely the most human-like of all bugs. Watch for them in late summer when they fly from place to place in fields and clearings.

**LENGTH:** about 50 mm.
**HABITAT:** open and shrubby areas.

# WALKING STICK

*Diapheromera femorata*

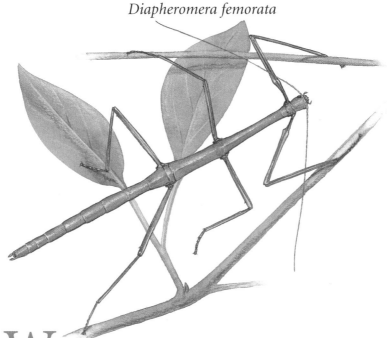

When the topic of insect camouflage comes up, the Walking Sticks are almost always the centre of attention. They do such a good job at appearing unbug-like. Not only is the body of a Walking Stick stick-like, the legs are too. As well, these insects will sometimes hold the front legs and antennae together in front of the small and inconspicuous head, further breaking up their buggish outline. Add to that their habit of walking rather slowly and deliberately, and Walking Sticks really do seem to disappear in plain sight.

There are many species of Walking Sticks around the world, but only one native to Canada. In Europe, and in Britain in particular, raising Walking Sticks is a popular hobby. The large tropical species are especially prized, and if you visit insect zoos, you'll see many of these tropical species here in Canada as well. It is,

> **LENGTH:** up to 100 mm.
> **HABITAT:** trees and shrubs, especially oak and raspberry.

however, illegal right now to keep non-native pet Walking Sticks on your own, because some species appear to have the potential to escape from captivity and become crop or garden pests.

# WOOD ROACH
*Parcoblatta pennsylvanica*

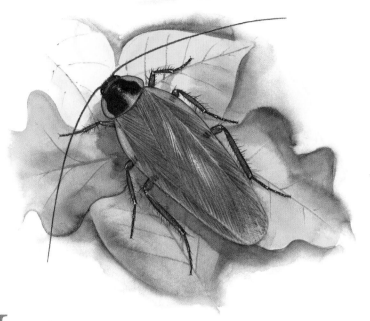

I t is unfortunate for the many thousands of species of harmless woodland cockroaches, living in the tropics around the world, that we temperate folks get such a poor introduction to the diversity and splendour of roaches as a group. The pesky cockroaches we find in Canada are all introduced species, and they are the only Canadian roaches capable of "infesting" houses and other buildings. Wood Roaches, on the other hand, live independent lives away from homes and green-houses. Like their relatives, they are active after dark and very difficult to catch. Their cerci (the two feelers on the end of the abdomen) can detect even the slightest breezes, and Wood Roaches instantly run when they feel the pressure wave of an approaching foot or hand.

**LENGTH:** about 25 mm.
**HABITAT:** leaf litter in forests and rocky areas.

Wood Roaches, by the way, are no more guilty of disease transmission than wood is. Note as well that the males have fully developed wings, while the wings of females are short and incapable of flight. The most northerly of all Wood Roaches, by the way, live in beaver houses near Rainier Lake, Ontario.

# EASTERN SUBTERRANEAN TERMITE

*Reticulitermes flavipes*

Termites are social insects, and young termites look much like the adults and serve as workers for the colony. The termite colony is made up of both males and females, unlike ants, bees and wasps, in which all the workers are female. When they mature, termites can be workers, soldiers or winged "reproductives." Unless you dig into their nests in rotting logs or underground, the termites you are most likely to encounter are the winged ones, on their late-summer flights. These flights are the means by which they find a mate and attempt to start a new colony.

Eastern Subterranean Termites forage at night, sometimes far from their nests. In some places they will construct mud tunnels in which to travel, protecting themselves from predators and from drying out. In Ontario, Eastern Subterranean Termites are found in the extreme south, as well as in the older parts of the city of Toronto.

> **LENGTH:** 5–10 mm.
> **HABITAT:** moist soil near wood, even in urban settings.

Termites eat wood, as anyone who lives in a wooden house knows, but they can't do it without some help. Approximately one third of their body weight is made up of microscopic protozoans. These "gut symbionts" digest cellulose in the wood.

# FIELD CRICKET
## *Gryllus veletis*

There is no more classic sound of summer than the chirping of crickets. Seeing one chirp, on the other hand, is no easy matter. If you do manage to get a peek, you'll find that it is only the males that make sound. Males can be identified by the two pointy things sticking out the back of their abdomen (the cerci), while females have three pointy things (two cerci and one egg-laying ovipositor). To make sounds, the male crickets rub their two wing-covers together, bringing a rasp into contact with a file. The hardened wing-covers amplify and resonate to produce the noise we all know and love. As for the old boy scout trick of counting the number of chirps per minute and using it to calculate the temperature (they chirp more slowly in the cold), this technique was actually worked out using a Tree Cricket's song (p. 114) and doesn't work well with Field Crickets. Carry a thermometer instead.

**LENGTH:** about 20 mm.
**HABITAT:** open areas.

If you don't mind horrific sights, Field Crickets can give a glimpse into the macabre world of insect parasitism. In most places, huge numbers of Field Crickets are infected with horsehair worms (in the phylum Nematomorpha), and if you place the crickets in very shallow water, the worms will emerge. It's really gross to watch, so don't say I didn't warn you!

# ROAD DUSTER

*Dissosteira carolina*

This is the signature grasshopper of vacant lots, construction sites, railway lines and gravel pits. In flight, this remarkable hopper looks like a Mourning Cloak butterfly (p. 37), with dark hind wings and a narrow, white or yellow border. As a young bug fanatic, I was fooled more than once by this resemblance. Recently, some entomologists have suggested that various band-winged grasshoppers (the subgroup to which the Road Duster belongs) resemble butterflies for a reason: the patterns on some butterflies may advertise to birds that the butterfly is a super-fast flyer, not worth pursuing. Other band-winged grasshoppers resemble sulphur butterflies, for the same reason. For the Road Dusters, the main defence when in flight is to simply drop to the ground and fold the wings. While on the ground, they are extremely difficult to see, what with their cinnamon brown

**LENGTH:** about 40 mm.
**HABITAT:** open places, especially disturbed ones such as vacant lots.

and grey bodies. They are so much like a dirt lump that even their eyes blend with the colour of the rest of the head.

Males do an interesting courtship display, called the hover flight. Watch for one to hover in mid-air, about a metre above the ground, fluttering the wings softly, first quickly and then at a slower speed.

111

# ANGULAR-WINGED KATYDID

*Microcentrum rhombifolium*

Katydids are wonderful plant mimics. They move slowly, on long, thin legs, and their wings and bodies really do look like green leaves. Some katydids go one step further, with fake bite marks on their wings or fake mould patches. Disguised among the leaves of the trees and shrubs in which they live, katydids carry out their leaf-eating lives. Males chirp to attract the females, and it is from the sound that one species makes that the name "katy-did" was derived, or at least that's what entomologists believe.

The katydids belong to a number of subgroups within a larger group of grigs called "Long-horned Grasshoppers." Indeed, katydids have long antennae, but some members of this gang are wingless, making them much less like a classic katydid than others. The Angular-winged Katydid (or Broad-winged Katydid, as it is sometimes called) is one of many katydid species in Ontario. It is native to the east, and it has recently colonized the west coast as well.

**LENGTH:** about 60 mm.
**HABITAT:** shrubs and trees.

# NORTHERN MOLE CRICKET

*Neocurtilla hexadactyla*

Mole crickets are diggers, like the moles they are named for. To look at them, you might not think they were a "cricket" at all, and actually, the name "cricket" is used rather loosely here. Mole crickets form a grig family of their own (the Gryllotalpidae, meaning "cricket moles," oddly enough) and are most abundant and diverse in the tropics.

Most of the time, a mole cricket stays hidden underground, but at night you will also find it at lightposts or house lights because it does fly. I'm always amazed that something that makes its living digging in the earth, without a full covering over the wings, can also fly, but it does. The front wings are shortened, and these wings are used to make chirping sounds, as in other crickets. The front legs are downright amazing, and worth a good close look with a magnifying glass. A bug couldn't ask for a better set of garden trowels. Mole crickets are also noteworthy for their parental care, and they do indeed look after their young underground for a short time following birth.

**LENGTH:** about 25 mm.
**HABITAT:** underground near water.

The Northern Mole Cricket is a rare bug in Ontario, found only in the extreme south.

# TREE CRICKET

*Oecanthus* spp.

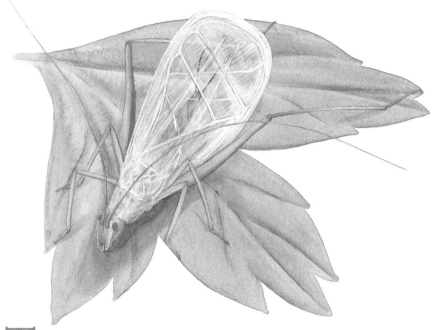

Tree Crickets are delicate, pale green creatures that sit up in trees or shrubs, singing thin but remarkably powerful songs. I like to look for them after dark with a flashlight, and if you don't bump the bush they are on, they will often keep singing, even with your nose a few centimetres from their bodies. The males are the noisy ones, as in all grigs, and when they sing, the front wings become a translucent blur. These are also easy insects to keep in captivity. As I write this account, I have one in a small plastic terrarium— I suppose I could track down a traditional oriental cricket cage, but I haven't looked for one yet—that sits in the kitchen of our house. Every evening, at about 8 p.m., the cricket begins to sing and fills the house with its sonic outpourings. In order to get to sleep, we have to close the door to the bedroom—the cricket is that loud! In the wild, wind noise and other grigs make them seem less noisy. I feed mine fruits and vegetables, by the way, and so far it has lived a bit more than two months.

**LENGTH:** about 15 mm.
**HABITAT:** shrubs and trees.

# EBONY JEWELWING

*Calopteryx maculata*

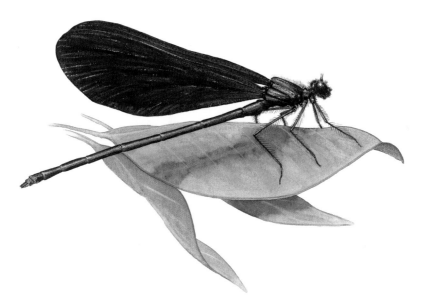

O f all the Canadian dragonflies and damselflies, this species is arguably the most beautiful. There is something simply elegant about the combination of a metallic blue-green body and jet black wings. The Ebony Jewelwing lives in lovely places as well. Its larvae prefers flowing waters and especially medium-sized streams through woodlands. When they emerge as adults, the males set up territories along the stream (or another nearby stream, I suppose), where they wait for females to pass by. Then, the males perform courtship displays, including throwing themselves into the water and drifting for a bit downstream.

In Europe, there is a similar species of jewelwing that has been studied extensively by insect behaviourists. Some of the finest documentary film-making I have ever seen is devoted to that species. In Ontario, if you see a jewelwing damselfly with only partly darkened wings (the tips are dark, the bases are not), it is the

**LENGTH:** about 60 mm.
**HABITAT:** along shady streams.

River Jewelwing (*C. aequabilus*), a separate species. It is only slightly less elegant in appearance and every bit as exciting to watch.

# EMERALD SPREADWING

*Lestes dryas*

These damselflies are mostly iridescent green, and as they get older, they develop a few bluish markings from a waxy powder, which is like the "bloom" on a plum. Damselfly specialists call this blue pigment "pruinosity," from the same word root as "prune."

The spreadwing damselflies are most common later in the summer, but the Emerald Spreadwing is the first member of this group to emerge, often sometime in June. Together, damselflies and dragonflies form the insect order Odonata, and unfortunately, we have no English term that refers to them both together. British people use the word "dragonfly" in this way, but it seems to me that giving "dragonfly" two confusingly similar meanings is a bad idea. I prefer the term "odonates" or just simply "odes" myself. Telling damselflies from dragonflies is easy: damselflies are thin, and all of their wings are similar in shape; dragonflies are more heavily built, and the hind wings are broader near the body than the front ones.

**LENGTH:** about 35 mm.
**HABITAT:** wetlands, often with forests nearby.

116

# BOREAL BLUET

*Enallagma boreale*

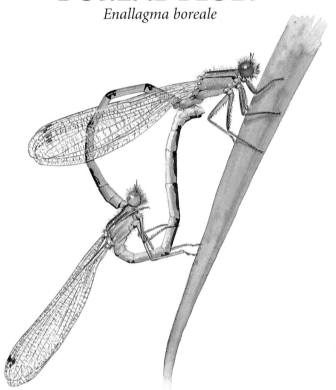

I f you have ever spent time beside a pond or a lake in May or June, you have seen these bluer-than-blue bugs. Like phosphorescent toothpicks, they hover among the reeds, where they catch their prey by plucking it off leaves while in flight. Aphids and baby grasshoppers are about the right size for a damselfly to tackle, and yes, Boreal Bluets are a type of damselfly. The males are patterned in blue and black, while some females are green or yellow instead of blue. To be honest, our species of American bluets all look more or less exactly alike. In cases like this, entomology books usually say something like "identification is best left to specialists." In reality, it's not that hard—all you need is a good magnifying glass and some obscure information. More and more, however, the popularity of damselfly and dragonfly watching is catching up to butterfly watching, which, in turn, is slowly catching up to bird watching.

**LENGTH:** about 32 mm.
**HABITAT:** ponds and lakes.

# SEDGE SPRITE

*Nehalennia irene*

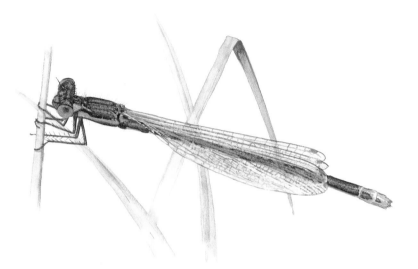

Probably our smallest damselfly, the Sedge Sprite is well named. It is spritely, and it is common in sedge-rich wetlands. Another tiny damselfly, the Eastern Forktail, is also common in these habitats, but the forktails are easy to tell from the sprites. Forktails have blue dots on the head, just behind the eyes, where sprites do not. In general, male damselflies are easier to tell apart than females, at least for people, but the damselflies have an interesting way of sorting each other out. On the very tip of the male's abdomen, he has a set of claspers, which fit perfectly on the back of the female's neck. When a male tries to mate with a female, he first attempts to get her in a headlock, so to speak. At this point, three things can happen. First, he can succeed, after which they fly away in tandem, mate and deposit the eggs. Second, the female may reject the male and evade his claspers with a bit of damselfly judo. Or third, the male may find that his claspers don't quite fit, which may be a sign that he has accosted the wrong species of female, or worse, another male.

**LENGTH:** about 30 mm.
**HABITAT:** ponds and lakes, often in low vegetation.

# GREEN DARNER

*Anax junius*

The Green Darner is not only big and beautiful, it is also a migrant. Each spring, Green Darners move northward with the warm weather, usually ensuring that they are the first large dragonflies to appear on the wing in any given location. They then breed in ponds and shallow lakes, and their progeny apparently hatch out before the autumn and stage a return migration south. At least that is what we think they do—no one has managed to mark and follow them, the way we do birds and Monarch butterflies (p. 42). Perhaps it is this migrating tendency that has made the Green Darner the most common and widespread large dragonfly in North America.

Male Green Darners are actually only green on the thorax—the abdomen is bright blue. In fact, the blue base of the male's abdomen is a good field mark, which makes this species easily recognizable at a distance. The female, on the other

> **LENGTH:** up to 80 mm.
> **HABITAT:** near ponds and lakes.

hand, is much more greenish looking, although her abdomen is actually greyish or brownish. As well, if you are lucky enough to see a dragonfly catch another dragonfly, or even a butterfly, this species is the one that is most likely to be involved.

# CANADA DARNER

*Aeshna canadensis*

The darners are our biggest dragonflies, and the Canada Darner is one of the most common of the group. Up close, the male is a dark brown insect, patterned in blue and green, usually with beautiful blue-green, black-spotted eyes. Some of the females are coloured this way, while others are brown and yellow. Darners spend most of the day on the wing, cruising the mid-summer skies for insects, which they capture in flight with their long, spiny legs. Darners breed in ponds and lakes, but they will also wander far from water to feed.

The name "darner," by the way, comes from the mistaken notion that these dragonflies will sew up your lips with their stinger. In reality, they have no stinger, and they don't sew, so put aside your fears. Some entomologists have suggested that this rumour got started when people wading in the shallows were accidentally jabbed by female darners, which were trying to lay eggs. I guess a bare leg is easy to mistake for a soft water plant. Darners are on the wing from late June all the way to the killing frosts of October.

**LENGTH:** 70 mm.
**HABITAT:** near ponds and lakes.

120

# RUSTY SNAKETAIL
*Ophiogomphus rupinsulensis*

M ost dragonflies live near ponds and lakes, because that is where their larvae grow up. However, most of the snaketails and other members of the clubtail family have larvae that live in rivers and streams.

The adults of this species are rarely common, and for dragonfly experts, they are always a thrill to see. Watch for a greenish dragonfly that sits on the ground, or on a bare branch, between flights. Up close, notice that the eyes of these dragonflies are widely separated, rather than touching one another in the middle of the head. Although the clubtail family is named for the expanded abdomenal tip of some of its members, the snaketails have only a modest "club." Notice as well

**LENGTH:** about 50 mm.
**HABITAT:** near streams.

that their coloration includes none of the intense blues and reds of other dragonflies. Instead, they are a lovely mint green. Green colour in animals is typically produced by a combination of yellow pigment and a blue "scattering" of light—the same thing that makes the sky blue. In other words, "Why is the sky blue" is a much simpler question than "Why is the snaketail green?"

# AMERICAN EMERALD

*Cordulia shurtleffi*

What a fine dragonfly this is! With gleaming green eyes and a jade black iridescent body, it has a certain style all its own. The American Emerald is our most common member of the emerald family, and it is a species of the early summer. It's hard to say whether emeralds or clubtails generate more excitement among dragonfly enthusiasts, but it's probably safe to say that the clubtails rule in the south, while the emeralds are symbols of the great northern forests. The American Emerald lays its eggs in ponds and small lakes, while other sorts of emeralds prefer boggy pools deep in black spruce and tamarack peatlands. The affinity of emeralds for boggy places contributes not only to their rarity but also to their appeal.

To get a good look at any of the emeralds, it really does help to catch them. Crouching by a skinny little brook as it flows through the muskeg below a beaver pond, the "odonatist" waits. Mosquitoes swarm by the dozens, but the stalker dares not swat them for fear of spooking a passing dragonfly. When one finally comes in reach, one swing of the net is all it will allow, and with it, you either bag the emerald or you do not.

**LENGTH:** about 45 mm.
**HABITAT:** ponds and lakes.

# COMMON WHITETAIL
*Libellula lydia*

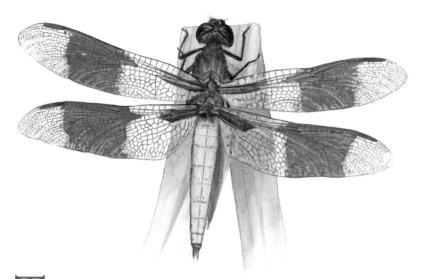

This dragonfly is a handsome animal, with a thick, muscular body and a broad, streamlined abdomen. When it is in the prime of its life, the abdomen of the male is a bright, shining beacon of white that serves to alert other dragonflies of its owner's presence. The female has an orange-brown abdomen, with less black on her wings.

You see the Common Whitetail mostly around ponds and lakes, and it seems to like patrolling along the reedy shoreline, landing from time to time on lookout perches, such as dead twigs or bent-over cattail stems. For most of us, the Common Whitetail is the dragonfly we associate most with farm ponds and other such dug-outs. This dragonfly seems to find such habitats quickly once they are constructed, and as a result, this species is widespread in North America. Males of many dragonfly species remain attached to the female while she lays eggs, so no other male can interrupt the egg-laying process. Female Common Whitetails, on the other hand, lay eggs by themselves, dipping their abdomen in the water while they fly.

**LENGTH:** about 45 mm.
**HABITAT:** ponds and lakes.

# YELLOW-LEGGED MEADOWHAWK

*Sympetrum vicinum*

For most people, there are two "kinds" of dragonflies in Ontario—the big, blue and/or green types and the little, red or yellow types. The blue and green dragonflies are, of course, darners, while the red or yellow species are mostly meadowhawks. The Yellow-legged Meadowhawk is one of our most common members of this group. Males have a deep red body, whereas females and young males are yellowish. You might not notice the yellow legs of this species, unless you reach the point where you want to recognize each of the 10 meadowhawks found in Ontario. With the growth of dragonfly watching as a hobby, this feat is not as unlikely as it may seem. Cherry-faced Meadowhawks, Black Meadowhawks, White-faced Meadowhawks and others all await you, and there are indeed good field guides that will help you tell them apart. Meadowhawks wander a great distance from their breeding ponds, and they show up in parks and gardens all the time. They like to perch on the ground or on low vegetation, so you can usually sneak up on them to get a good look.

**LENGTH:** about 38 mm.
**HABITAT:** open areas, ponds and lakes.

# MAYFLY LARVAE
## Order Ephemeroptera

Some kinds of bugs seem to exist only for the sake of getting eaten by other creatures. Of course, this isn't true, but it sure seems that way. Mayflies and their larvae are one such group, and they are about as defenceless as a bug can get.

The one pictured here is part of a group of Mayfly Larvae called "crawlers." The other 100–200 species of mayflies in this part of the world are either crawlers, burrowers or swimmers. Each has its own style of feeding, and they all eat things like algae and detritus. Some use their hairy front feet to strain food from the water. Some Mayfly Larvae live in streams, some in ponds, some in lakes and some in rivers. The easiest way to recognize them is by their three-pronged abdomen tip, and the fuzzy gills that line the sides of their abdomen. When mayflies emerge as adults, they generally live only a single day. When they first emerge, they are called "duns" or "subimagos"—an odd stage that no other insect goes through. They then shed their skin again, wings and all, and become the short-lived true adult that lives only long enough to mate and lay eggs.

**LENGTH:** up to 30 mm.
**HABITAT:** water, especially streams and rivers.

# DAMSELFLY LARVA
## Order Odonata, Suborder Zygoptera

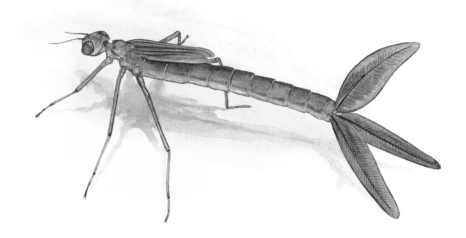

Here's an odd critter. At the back end of its long, slender body, you see three things that look like dead leaves. These are the insect's gills, with which it takes oxygen from the water. Six long legs help it scramble among the underwater plants, where it watches for prey with its bulging compound eyes. When a small, edible insect is spotted, the larva takes aim and ... schnik! The folded lower lip shoots out, many times the length of the larva's head, and grabs the unlucky prey like the tongue of a chameleon lizard. Damselfly Larvae are common in ponds and lakes, and they are easy to recognize. They are not good swimmers, mind you, and when they do have to swim, they wiggle through the water like a person with their hands at their sides. If you look closely at the top of a Damselfly Larva's thorax, you'll see four little wing pads. These wing pads will eventually become the adult damselfly's wings, when the larva finally climbs up out of the water and sheds its skin for the final time.

**LENGTH:** up to 29 mm.
**HABITAT:** most common in ponds and "weedy" lakes.

# DRAGONFLY LARVA
## Order Odonata, Suborder Anisoptera

Damselfly Larvae are weird, but Dragonfly Larvae are even weirder. Both have the folding lower lip that catches prey, and both have big eyes and slender legs, but there the similarities seem to end. Dragonfly Larvae are bigger, heavier and more powerful than Damselfly Larvae (p. 126). As well, instead of leaf-like gills, they keep their gills inside the end of their abdomen, in their rectum. That means, I'm afraid, that they breathe with their butt. And when they need to swim, what do they do? They squirt water out their back end, and shoot through the pond with jet propulsion.

The larvae of the darner dragonflies (pp. 119–20) are long and stream-lined, like the one shown above. Skimmer Dragonfly Larvae have longer legs and fatter bodies, sometimes with lots of spikes out the sides. Often, they become covered with algae and pond "guck." Perhaps the oddest Dragonfly Larvae are the snaketails that spend their lives partly buried in mud at the bottom of streams and rivers and have smaller eyes and shorter legs. No matter what the species, Dragon-

**LENGTH:** up to 50 mm.
**HABITAT:** ponds, lakes and streams.

fly Larvae take at least a few months to grow up, and when they emerge to become adults, they crawl up on plants or on the sandy banks of rivers.

# SALMONFLY LARVA

*Pteronarcys* spp.

A t first, the larva of a Salmonfly (*P. californica*) might look a lot like a great big Mayfly Larva (p. 125), but look closely and notice the differences. Salmonflies are a type of stonefly, and stoneflies form an insect order separate from the mayflies. A Stonefly Larva has only two long feelers on the end of its abdomen, whereas a mayfly usually has three. The Stonefly Larva will keep this feature as an adult, and an adult stonefly looks a whole lot like a larva, except with wings. When the biggest of our stoneflies emerge as adults, fishermen call them "salmonflies," and trout go wild trying to eat as many as possible while the feast lasts. Stoneflies don't live in ponds or lakes—they only like streams and rivers. Even then, they seem to prefer clear, fast-flowing water, with lots of dissolved oxygen. Unlike Mayfly Larvae, which have gills on the sides of their abdomens, Stonefly Larvae gills are tucked into their leg pits, so to speak. Without a powerful magnifying glass, and an upside-down larva, they are tough to see.

**LENGTH:** up to 50 mm.
**HABITAT:** along rivers.

What do Stonefly Larvae eat? Mostly water plants and algae, much like Caddisfly Larvae (p. 130) and Water Scavenger Beetles (p. 140), but some are predators. With their powerful legs, they hold onto underwater rocks and fight the current that threatens to sweep them away.

# WATER TIGER

*Dytiscus* spp.

The Water Tiger is really just the larva of the Giant Diving Beetle (p. 138), and other sorts of diving beetles have similar larvae, too. This connection leads some people to confuse the diving beetles and the tiger beetles, but tiger beetles live only on land and never in the water.

A Water Tiger is a marvellous beast. It swims with all six legs and in a very graceful fashion, floating almost effortlessly through the pond. On its broad, flat head, the Water Tiger has eyes, but they are simple eyes, not the large compound eyes of the adults. As well, whereas the adults kill their prey by chewing on it with

**LENGTH:** up to 60 mm.
**HABITAT:** ponds, lakes and streams.

short but powerful jaws, the jaws of the Water Tiger are like two hypodermic needles. The Water Tiger swims up to its prey and then attacks quickly and savagely. Once a fish or tadpole has been impaled, digestive juices are injected, and the prey dissolves in its own body. You might think Water Tigers are some of the most fearsome creatures in the pond, but they often fall prey to both Giant Water Bugs (p. 133) and the adults of their own species.

Most Water Tigers prefer to eat small vertebrates, but some are more fond of eating insects instead. Like the adults, Water Tigers have to come to the surface to breathe, and their breathing hole is located right at the tip of their abdomen.

# CADDISFLY LARVAE
### Order Trichoptera

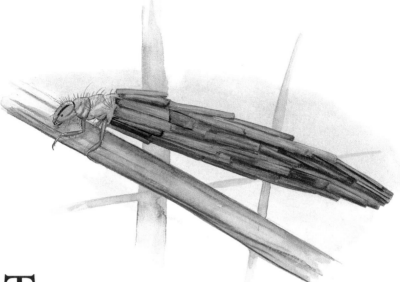

To most people, an adult caddisfly doesn't quite qualify as a "cool" bug. They are moth-like and only moderately colourful, and the only obvious things that set them apart from other bugs are their wispy, long antennae. But every caddisfly was once a larva, and Caddisfly Larvae are just plain nifty.

Most Caddisfly Larvae are scavengers, but some eat algae, which they graze from rocks and water plants. While they are doing this, they are constantly at risk from all of the underwater predators around them. So, they protect themselves with cases—coverings for their soft, grub-like bodies. Some make the cases from twigs, while others use pebbles, reeds or leaves, which are held together with silk and saliva. Most cases are straight, but some are coiled like a snail shell.

To find Caddisfly Larvae, look into a shallow pond and watch the bottom. Pretty soon, you'll see things move that you thought were just debris. These are the larva cases. Trout eat many of these insects, by the way, and experiments have shown that they recognize Caddisfly Larvae by looking for their eyes. "If it has eyes, it must be alive" is the trout's rule, and when you think of it, that's not a bad way to find bugs yourself.

**LENGTH:** with case, up to 60 mm.
**HABITAT:** ponds, lakes, rivers and streams.

# GOLDEN MAYFLY

*Hexagenia* spp.

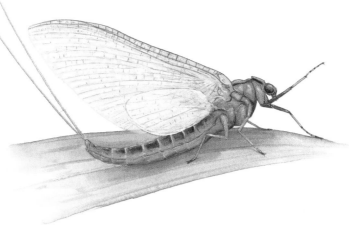

Mayfly adults are not really aquatic, but their activities on land are so short lived that I have included them here. When an adult mayfly emerges from its larval skin and flies up to the vegetation near the water body in which it developed, the clock begins to tick. It sheds its skin for a second time, wings and all, and then begins its search for a mate. Most mayflies form swarms in the air, where males congregate and females go to find a male. After this event, the males simply die. The females, with only hours to live, return to the water from whence they came and flop down into the water to lay eggs. Because the adult females are called "spinners" by anglers, this is the celebrated "spinner fall" that brings trout to the surface, in what is usually called the "evening rise."

**LENGTH:** 20–30 mm.
**HABITAT:** near water.

The Golden Mayfly is not only one of our most abundant species, it is also one of the largest. These mayflies are attracted to lights (as are most mayflies), and when a really big emergence is underway, they can pile up under a good light (as opposed to a yellowish, bug-proof light) in amazing numbers.

131

# EASTERN KAYAK POND SKATER

*Limnoporus dissortis*

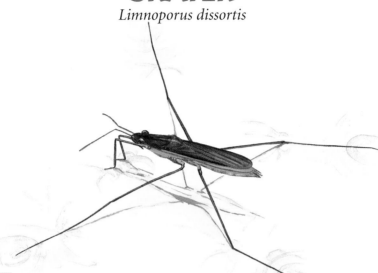

Let's face it—it's just plain weird that an animal can live on the surface of the water without falling through. Pond skaters (also called water striders) do this in a fascinating way. Four of their legs are very long and distribute the weight of their slender bodies over a large area of the water's surface. The water itself has a sort of skin to it—the "surface tension"—that is strong enough to support an insect, but only if its legs repel water, which naturally a pond skater's do.

**LENGTH:** about 13 mm.
**HABITAT:** ponds and lakes.

For these little bugs, the surface of a pond must feel like a great, slippery waterbed mattress, stretching off in all directions. On this bizarre playing field pond skaters search for food in the form of other bugs that have fallen in and drowned or are in the process of drowning. Because pond skaters are sucking bugs, they have the same sort of piercing proboscis that allows their aquatic relatives to overpower and consume their own buggy prey.

Eastern Kayak Pond Skaters have wings, but the adults of many of their relatives are wingless. Winged pond skaters can leave one pond and settle elsewhere, while those that are wingless must be satisfied with their humble pool and trust that things will remain to their liking.

# GIANT WATER BUG
*Lethocerus americanus*

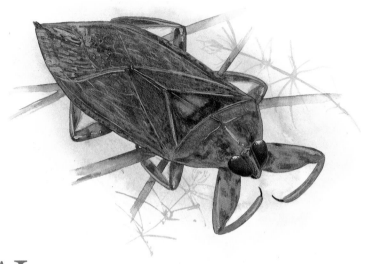

With its swollen forearms, this critter is the bodybuilder of the pond world. Oddly enough, it also looks like a domino-sized piece of wet brown cardboard. In flight, a Giant Water Bug looks a lot like a small bat, and these insects are attracted to lights at night.

Once a Giant Water Bug grasps a luckless fish, tadpole or fellow insect, the result is inevitable. The sucking beak plunges deep, and digestive juices are injected. Because of these enzymes, the prey dissolves inside its own body, while the willow leaf–sized insect holds on and waits until the time is right to suck. When the meal is done, the bug swims off to digest, using two pairs of swimming legs, not one. After all, it is our largest aquatic insect, and it needs the extra power to propel its hefty body through the water.

**LENGTH**: 50 mm.
**HABITAT**: ponds and lakes, sometimes rivers.

Young Giant Water Bugs look much like the adults, but without wings. These impressive creatures can be found in still or slow-flowing waters, and they are most abundant in cattail marshes. And yes, if one bites you, it really does hurt, although they don't go out of their way to bite people.

133

# WATER BOATMAN
## Famiy Corixidae

Although small, Water Boatmen are amazing. Take a look at their legs. The first pair are shaped like little garden trowels, and the bug uses them for sifting through muck for food. The next pair are long and pointed, and the boatman uses them to hold onto plants or rocks while underwater. Then there are the back legs, which are the boatman's oars.

**LENGTH:** 4–10 mm.
**HABITAT:** most waterbodies, but rare in fast streams.

If you keep a Water Boatman in a glass jar, you can see how it breathes underwater. A layer of air clings to the boatman's tummy, and it breathes from this bubble. The oxygen the bug needs enters the bubble from the surrounding water. At the same time, carbon dioxide leaves the bubble and goes into the pond. Slowly, the bubble gets smaller as nitrogen dissolves into the water, and then the bug pops to the surface to replenish its air supply.

Water Boatmen live in ponds, rivers, lakes and even saline sloughs. At times, there can be millions of them in one place, and when they accidentally fly to lights at night, they can cover the ground with their bodies.

# COMMON BACKSWIMMER

*Notonecta undulata*

Are you any good at the backstroke? Well, it seems that the backswimmer doesn't know any other way to swim. At first, you might think that a Common Backswimmer is just an upside-down Water Boatman (p. 134), but have another look. Both pairs of front legs are short and stocky, for grabbing prey, and instead of resting on underwater plants, backswimmers scull around up at the surface of the pond. They rest with their legs touching the underside of the water surface and their heads aimed slightly downward, ready to dive.

**LENGTH:** 11 mm.
**HABITAT:** ponds, lakes and slower rivers and streams.

If you catch a backswimmer and flip it over, you'll see how pretty it is, with bright white wings and fiery red eyes. Don't let it bite you though! The bite of a backswimmer is like that of a Giant Water Bug (p. 133)—intended to dissolve your flesh. People who keep fish in outdoor ponds dread backswimmers, because they eat a lot of small fishes, as well as other bugs. In nature, however, they are both the predator and the prey, and they make the world of the pond more interesting, even if it is a bit more dangerous.

# WATER SCORPION
*Ranatra fusca*

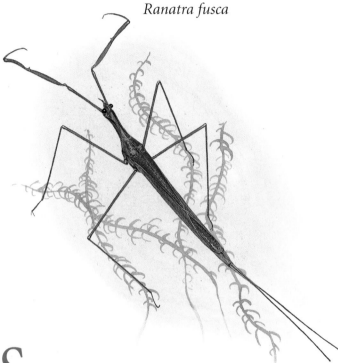

Structurally, a Water Scorpion is built almost exactly like a Giant Water Bug (p. 133), but on a much slimmer plan. To look at them, however, you'd think you were gazing at an underwater praying mantid. Water Scorpions do indeed catch their buggy prey with their forelegs, the way mantids do, but their forelegs are not spiked, and their heads do not swivel in all directions the way a mantid's head does. As well, they have piercing, sucking mouthparts, rather than the chewing mouthparts of mantids.

**LENGTH:** up to 30 mm, not counting the breathing tube.
**HABITAT:** ponds and lakes.

Amazingly, Water Scorpions can get up out of the water and fly to a new pond when the need arises. Or at least the adults can—young Water Scorpions look much like their parents, but without wings. Water Scorpions breathe through a siphon that extends out the back of their abdomens. It is not a tube, but rather two parallel rods of cuticle with water-repellent hairs on them. Because the surface tension of the water cannot penetrate the hairs, the siphon acts like a tube, even though it is not solid.

# MID-SIZED DIVING BEETLE
*Colymbetes sculptilis*

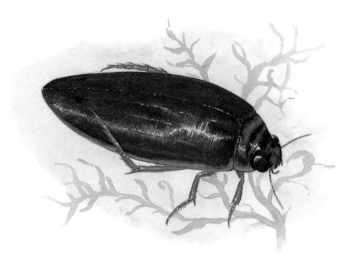

Mid-sized Diving Beetles commonly fly to meltwater ponds, and they don't mind living for a while in places that are nothing more than flooded playgrounds. There, they chase down Water Boatmen (p. 134) and other small bugs, and chew them to pieces with their strong jaws. You might even find one on top of a car on a sunny day. To the beetles, a shiny car looks like a small pond, and when they fly down to dive into the water, they suddenly find them-

**LENGTH**: 13 mm.
**HABITAT**: ponds, rain pools, meltwater pools and lakes.

selves upside-down on a hot metal roof. Diving beetles have trouble flipping over once they are on their backs, and they also find it tough to take flight on land. Many of them die on hot cars as a result, unable to escape.

If you look very closely at a Mid-sized Diving Beetle, you'll see that it is smooth, but that it also has hundreds of very fine lines running crosswise on the top of its wing-covers (a good way to recognize this species). If you find one that looks right but is about half the size, it is probably one of the Rhantus Diving Beetles (*Rhantus* spp.)—also interesting and also common in meltwater ponds.

# GIANT DIVING BEETLE

*Dytiscus* spp.

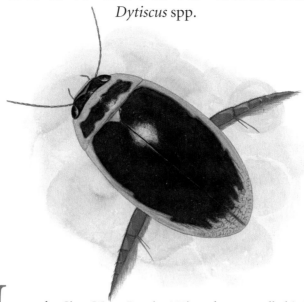

Next to the Giant Water Bug (p. 133), and some really big Dragonfly Larvae (p. 127), Giant Diving Beetles are our biggest aquatic insects. They are powerful predators that will eat almost anything they can over-power. If you keep pond critters in an aquarium, you will find that sooner or later there is only one left, and in most cases the survivor will be either a Giant Water Bug or a Giant Diving Beetle. The Alaskan Giant Diving Beetle (*D. alaskanus*) is one of our common species, but it is also one of the small-est. The most impressive member of this group is the Harris's Diving Beetle (*D. harrisii*)—a big one can be 40 mm long!

In most species, female Giant Diving Beetles come in two forms: the first form looks a lot like the male, with shiny, black wing-covers; the second form has grooves running the length of the wing-covers, making it look at first glance like it must be a different species. A female with a white blob on the end of her abdomen has been mated—the white stuff discourages other males from mating with her again. Males have round sucker pads on their front feet, for holding onto the females. If you notice a bad smell when handling these beetles, it is probably their defence chemicals. These steroids are powerful, and predators respect them.

**LENGTH:** 27 mm.
**HABITAT:** ponds, lakes and some-times slower rivers.

# WHIRLIGIG BEETLE

*Dineutus* spp.

These water beetles are probably the coolest of them all. With the most efficient swimming legs in the entire animal world, they zip around on top of the water, spinning and whirring like super-fast bumper cars. If they need to, they can dive underwater. They also have wings when the time comes to find a new pond. Sometimes, thousands of Whirligig Beetles band together to form a flotilla on the surface.

**LENGTH:** up to 10 mm.
**HABITAT:** ponds and lakes.

If you have a microscope, and a Whirligig Beetle specimen, you can see how amazing its eyes are. Each eye is actually split in two! One half looks up into the air, while the other half watches down into the water. Of course, while they are spinning and whirring at high speed, their eyes need all the help they can get, so they also use their short, triangular antennae to "feel" their way through the twists and turns.

Whirligig Beetles are predators, and they will eat any unfortunate bug they can catch on the water's surface. Even baby pond skaters (p. 132) are not fast enough to get away from them. If another animal tries to eat a Whirligig, it gets a mouthful of something that smells a lot like rotting fruit. Half-sized versions of this beetle are still Whirligigs, by the way, in the genus *Gyrinus*.

# WATER SCAVENGER BEETLE
*Hydrophilus triangularis*

Finally, a water beetle that isn't a ferocious predator. Water Scavenger Beetles are the gentle ones in the water beetle crowd, and they feed on plants and various sorts of debris. When they swim, they paddle like crazy with all six legs, but most of the time they cling to underwater plants. In many ways, Water Scavenger Beetles look like they are trying to pretend they are not underwater at all, behaving more like leaf beetles on the willows by the shore.

**LENGTH:** about 35 mm.
**HABITAT:** ponds and lakes.

For Water Scavenger Beetles, life is careful and slow. For diving beetles, it is risky and fast. Whereas the diving beetles keep their air supply under their wings, hidden from view, the Water Scavenger Beetles keep air both under the wings and all along their undersides. Underwater, they look like they are coated with liquid mercury. To replenish the bubble, they don't just bob to the surface either. Instead, they just barely stick their heads up and allow the air to flow around their antennae.

This species is the biggest Water Scavenger Beetle in North America. Smaller types abound, mind you, and the large ones are certainly not typical of their family.

# SOW BUG

*Oniscus aselus*

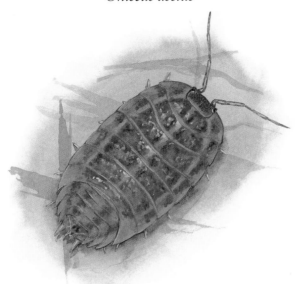

In general, insects are the bugs of the land, while crustaceans are the bugs of the sea. Some crustaceans, however, live on land, but they can only survive in moist places because they breathe with modified gills. Crabs are crustaceans, and many people are familiar with the air-breathing hermit crabs that are such popular critters in pet stores. Even marine crabs can spend a fair amount of time out of the water, up on rocks or sand.

Sow Bugs were accidentally introduced from—where else?—Europe. It is interesting that European bugs generally do well when they are introduced to North America, while the reverse is rarely true. Sow Bugs are sometimes confused with Pill Bugs (*Armadillidium vulgare*), but Pill Bugs roll up into a ball when they

> **LENGTH:** about 10 mm.
> **HABITAT:** most common in gardens and leaf litter.

are frightened, whereas Sow Bugs do not. Both bugs are slow-moving, heavily armoured creatures that are easily recognized by their many legs and their many-segmented shell of a body. They are not harmful, and they feed only on decaying material, both plant and animal. Because our gardens are almost completely unnatural ecosystems to begin with, the addition of Sow Bugs and Pill Bugs is not much different from adding another two species of non-native flowering plants.

# GARDEN CENTIPEDE

*Lithobius* sp.

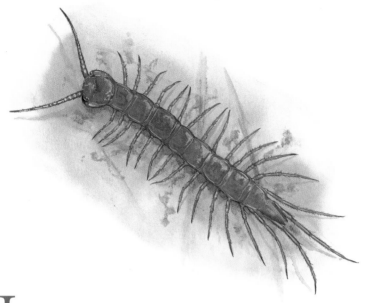

Lift a board, or turn the soil in your average Ontario garden, and you're likely to find a centipede. The typical specimen is about 25 mm long and rusty orange in colour. Centipedes move rapidly, twist like miniature snakes and can squeeze into what seem like the tiniest openings to escape. This ability is probably why you also find them in basements so often. A slight opening between a window and the foundation or a crack between wood and cement will allow them to get in. Once in a building, however, centipedes are no longer in contact with their most cherished substance—moisture. They dry out quickly indoors, and when you find them, they are usually desiccated and shrivelled to about half their normal size.

**LENGTH:** up to about 30 mm.
**HABITAT:** moist soil, leaf litter and lawns.

Centipedes are predators, and they have venomous fangs that they use to subdue their prey. Our species are not dangerous to people, but I still advise small children to avoid handling them. If you can get a centipede to sit still for a moment, you'll see that each body segment carries one pair of legs, and the legs are set off to the sides. In contrast, each segment of a millipede bears two legs, which are set underneath.

# ROUND MILLIPEDE

Order Julida

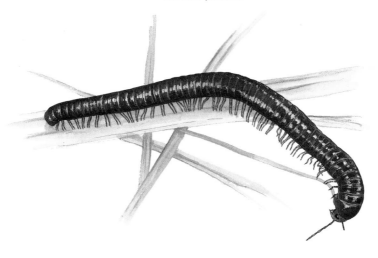

The main similarity between a millipede and a centipede is that their names end in "-pede," a word root that refers to their feet. Big millipedes, at least in this part of the world, are bigger than big centipedes. A millipede has many more legs than a centipede because it bears two pairs of legs on each body

> **LENGTH:** up to 100 mm.
> **HABITAT:** on the ground in a variety of places.

segment, compared to a centipede's one. The antennae on a millipede's head give it a somewhat insect-like appearance from the neck forward, and, indeed, the science of animal classification places millipedes closer to insects than centipedes.

Millipedes are slow-moving animals that feed on plants or detritus. The great joy in finding a millipede is watching it walk. Because there are so many legs, they run the risk of getting in each other's way. To avoid such a calamity, the millipede moves its legs in slow, coordinated waves, starting at the back of the body and moving toward the head.

For those of you who know that millipede means "thousand foot" while centipede means "hundred foot," please make a note that millipedes always have fewer than 1000 feet, and centipedes can have as few as 30. A 100-footed centipede is actually an impossibility, because they always have an odd number of leg pairs. The closest it can get is 98 (49 x 2) or 102 (51 x 2).

143

# HARVESTMAN
## Order Opiliones

I used to call these creatures "daddy long-legs," and as a kid I thought they were spiders. I now try to use the more traditional name "harvestman" to refer to them, because just about any long-legged bug gets called a daddy long-legs. You can tell that Harvestmen are not spiders because, unlike spiders, they have no constriction between the head and the abdomen. Harvestmen are also unable to produce silk. Their eyes are set in a little mound on the top of the body, and the eight legs extend out from the sides.

**LENGTH:** about 5 mm, without the legs.
**HABITAT:** gardens, fields and forests.

These critters are predatory, although, as you might imagine, they are no match for anything but small prey. They will also scavenge on dead bugs or bits of decaying plants. Because Harvestmen are such familiar garden bugs, various odd beliefs have developed about them. Some people believe that they are extremely venomous, even though it is tough to get them to bite. As far as I can determine, this story is complete baloney. Another weird story has to do with the belief that if your cow goes missing, you pull off a Harvestman's leg and throw it on the ground, where it will point you in the right direction.

# WOLF SPIDER
*Lycosa* spp.

Wolf Spiders are wandering hunters, and although they do not spin a web, they can still produce silk from the "spinneret" glands on their abdomen. Most of the time, you will see them in grassy places, where they search for other bugs. They are easy to find day or night, and if you search for them with a head lamp

> **LENGTH:** up to 10 mm.
> **HABITAT:** open and grassy places.

(not a flashlight), you'll see their eyes gleaming in the grass, like little points of dew. The trick is to go out looking on a dry night, when there is no dew to confuse you!

Wolf Spiders have moderately good vision, and they can also see the patterns of polarized light in the sky, which helps them find their way around their grassy little worlds. Females are bigger than the males, and when they lay eggs, they wrap them in a silk bag. The female spider attaches the bag to her spinnerets and carries the eggs with her until they hatch. She then looks like an even bigger spider with a blue abdomen, the blue part really being the egg sac, of course. When the young hatch, they cling to the body of their mother, holding onto special handle hairs on her back.

# BOLD JUMPER
*Phidippus audax*

Even people with a deep-seated fear of spiders sometimes see a glimmer of cuteness in the members of the jumping spider family. Sure, they have eight legs and eight eyes, but they don't move in the same creepy way that other spiders do. Instead, they walk around in a more insect-like fashion (if that means anything to you), and they also jump. When you look at one up close,

**LENGTH:** up to 10 mm.
**HABITAT:** sunny, open places.

most of the time it will turn and look back with the pair of big, bright eyes on the front of its head. Jumping spiders have the best vision of any spiders, and they can swivel their head around to examine whatever catches their interest. Add to this the fact that some, such as the Boreal Jumping Spider (*P. borealis*), have colourful bodies and iridescent green fangs, and you have a spider with both a "face" and a personality. Many of the smaller jumping spiders also do complicated little courtship dances, waving their fangs, their pedipalps (the little leggish things in front of the fangs) and their front legs, like coloured flags. If the female likes the dance, she will mate with the male.

# NORTHERN BLACK WIDOW
*Lactrodectus variolus*

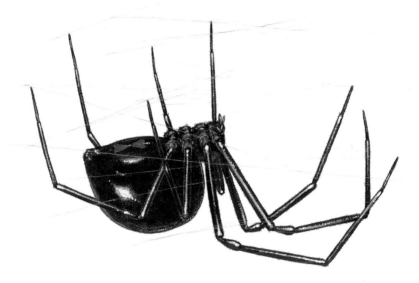

B lack widows in Ontario? Absolutely, but only on the Bruce Peninsula. The best way to see one is to walk around open areas in mid-summer and shine a flashlight down old mammal burrows, which usually are easy to find. The black widow spins a disorganized web, and it is just about the easiest spider in Ontario to identify: shiny black with a red hourglass on its tummy. The venom of these

> **LENGTH:** females to 12 mm; males to 5 mm.
> **HABITAT:** nooks and crannies.

beasts can indeed be deadly, but fortunately they are shy and docile most of the time. In keeping with their name, the females do eat the males quite often after mating. This trait is actually fairly common among spiders, and it is not the macabre ritual that some people imagine.

Apart from mammal burrows, the best place to look for black widows is in the grocery store, because many of them come in with fruits and vegetables. Sometimes they have a different pattern of red or orange markings on their backs, indicating they came from the southern US. If you see a smaller spider with a smudgy, orange-brown mark on its tummy, don't be fooled; it is the Boreal Cobweb Spider (*Steatoda borealis*).

# SHAMROCK ORB-WEAVER

*Aranaeus trifolium*

This spider is one that makes the classic "orb" web we all know and love—flat, with radiating spokes and a spiral of silk connecting them together. If you have never watched a spider make a web, you really owe it to yourself to do so. If nothing else, it is fascinating to think of how wondrous it is that any animal could do something so complex based on nothing but pre-programmed instinct. Because humans are among the few animals with almost no innate behaviour patterns (except perhaps things like smiling or yawning), we really can't imagine what it is like. The spider spins a perfect web every time, and it knows exactly how to move around on it holding the non-sticky threads while the prey get caught in the sticky ones.

**LENGTH:** up to 11 mm.
**HABITAT:** shrubs, trees and the sides of buildings.

Tossing small insects into an orb-weaver's web is standard practice for outdoor kids, and we've all seen the spider wrap up its prey in silk and then deliver the death-fanging that injects the poison. These spiders also show us how easy it is for the average person to completely ignore an interesting sort of "bug"—only when they grow to full size do people notice them, and every entomologist gets phone calls in autumn asking "What *is* this thing?"

# YELLOW GARDEN SPIDER

*Argiope aurantia*

This spider, the star of the book *Charlotte's Web*, is also a common image at Halloween and a very familiar sight to any camper or gardener. The Yellow Garden Spider is both colourful and large, and it is an impressive creature any way you look at it. In most respects, it is a typical member of the orb-weaver family, but it does have some fascinating characteristics of its own.

An interesting feature of its web is the X-shaped, white silk "stabilimentum" at its centre. It was originally thought to be a strengthening device that stabilized the web (hence the name), but arachnologists have wondered more recently if it helps protect the web from damage by flying birds. The big female spider

> **LENGTH:** about 10–15 mm.
> **HABITAT:** shrubby and open areas, moist meadows.

typically sits right in the middle of the web, with her legs aligned with the four arms of the stabilimentum. Perhaps this pose makes the spider easier to see and birds less likely to accidentally fly into the web, which would only mean more work for both the spider and the bird. Yellow Garden Spiders do not always sit in the web, however, and they generally have a nearby silk hideaway under a leaf or behind a plant stem.

# ARROW-SHAPED MICRATHENA

*Micrathena sagittata*

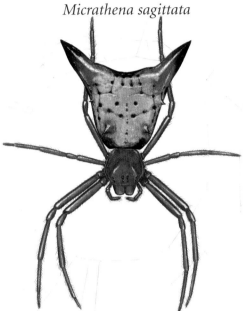

O K, it's not exactly arrow-shaped (arrow*head*-shaped, maybe), but it's a cool spider nonetheless. Most spiders are actually quite soft-bodied as bugs go, but this one is equipped with hardened spines on its abdomen. The spines make the spider not only look less like a spider, but also harder to eat.

The Arrow-shaped Micrathena is a member of the orb-weaving spider family (Aranaeidae), and it is not the only one with hardened spines. The spines do not get in the way of web-making, and it spins a perfectly normal, flat "orb" web, with which it catches flying insects in the perfectly normal (although amazing) orb-weaver fashion. The main thing that distinguishes the web of this species from those of its relatives is the fact that it has a hole in the centre. This hole is where the spider sits and waits for prey. When a bug hits the web, the spider then has a choice between running out to greet its meal on the front or the back of the web (if indeed webs do have fronts and backs). When you think of it, it is odd that other spiders haven't developed this same habit.

**LENGTH:** up to 10 mm.
**HABITAT:** clearings, parks and gardens, particularly in the Windsor area.

# SIX-SPOTTED FISHING SPIDER

*Dolomedes triton*

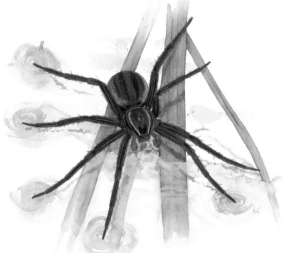

I f you read a lot of nature books, you'll eventually see photographs of these spiders eating small fishes, but personally I have never witnessed it. These spiders live in ponds and can walk on the water like a water strider (so it seems quite natural that they would eat small fishes). The fishing spiders let their heavy

> **LENGTH:** females to 15 mm; males to 10 mm.
> **HABITAT:** ponds and small lakes.

bellies lay on the surface because they can't quite support their weight on tiptoes. They crawl around on underwater plants, breathing from air trapped in the tiny hairs that cover their body and legs.

However, I once worked in a lab where we studied these spiders, and none of the arachnologists I worked with ever saw one get a fish! The spiders ate lots of water striders, damselflies and bugs that fell into the water, but no fishes. Maybe it happens more often in other places, or maybe those photographs were posed. Female fishing spiders are bigger than the males and often eat the males during or after courtship. Females who have already mated are less patient with suitors, so males sometimes follow immature females, waiting for them to reach adulthood. When the female lays her eggs, she carries them in a silk bag in her jaws, unlike wolf spiders, which carry them on their spinnerets.

# FLOWER SPIDER
*Misumena vatia*

H ere's the scenario: a big fat spider waits patiently in a fresh blossom. Sometimes the spider is yellow and sometimes it is white, and sometimes these colours blend in perfectly with the flowers, while other times they don't. An insect comes to the flower for a sip of nectar, and suddenly it becomes spider fodder.

My favourite story about this spider involved a butterfly, a male blue. The blue was flitting about in the greenery, stopping from time to time to sun itself, when it spied another blue. It flapped over to investigate, but the second butterfly seemed completely uninterested. That's when I saw the female Flower Spider, which was tucked up between the purple flowers of the vetch they were all on. Before the first blue could comprehend the situation (if ever it could at all), the spider reached out, grabbed it and had two blues for lunch instead of one. Not only had the spider used the flower as an ambush, it had also used the first blue as a decoy!

**LENGTH:** females about 8 mm; males about 3 mm.
**HABITAT:** flowers in meadows and fields.

Males of this species are smaller and darker than the females. In a wild rose flower, the males look almost exactly like the pollen-bearing stamens—the best spider camouflage I know of in Ontario!

# BOOKS FOR BUGSTERS

Unlike birds or mammals, there is no one "book" that covers the entire bug fauna of Ontario or any other state, province or country for that matter. You must be ready to face the fact that we have a great deal of knowledge about a few selected groups of bugs and almost no knowledge of all the others.

It is sad that almost all the references that follow are out of print or hard to find. Hopefully, we will soon see an improvement in the funding and support that "faunistic" studies receive. Let's hope that the work of detailing our arthropod fauna grows more and more vibrant in the new millennium, whether it is led by amateurs or professionals, or people like me, on the border between the two.

The following books will take you a few steps further in your understanding of local bugs. I have avoided isolated papers in entomological journals, but if you are serious in your quest, these references will quickly lead you to them as well. I should also mention two important series of books. The first is entitled "Insects and Arachnids of Canada," and it was published by Agriculture Canada in Ottawa. It covers some of the spiders, beetles, two-winged flies and sucking bugs. Unfortunately, this series lost its funding before covering the entire Canadian fauna. The second is "The Moths of America North of Mexico, Including Greenland," and it is published by E.W. Classey Ltd. and R.B.D. Publications. It does not yet cover all of our moths, but the plan is to eventually treat each and every species.

You might also try searching the worldwide web for information on specific sorts of bugs. As usual, some of it is well-researched and helpful while most is not. Some groups, such as dragonflies, enjoy much better coverage on the web than others.

## BOOKS

Arnett, Ross H., Jr., 1985. *American Insects: A Handbook of the Insects of America North of Mexico.* Van Nostrand Reinhold Company, New York.

Bartlett Wright, Amy. 1993. *Peterson First Guide to Caterpillars of North America.* Houghton Mifflin Co., Boston and New York.

Bousquet, Yves, editor. 1991. *Checklist of Beetles of Canada and Alaska.* Agriculture Canada, Ottawa.

Catling, P.M., and V.R. Brownell. 2000. *Damselflies and Dragonflies of Ontario: Resource Guide and Annotated List.* Proresources, Metcalfe, Ontario.

Chu, H.F., and Laurence K. Cutkomp. 1992. *How to Know the Immature Insects. Pictured Key Nature Series.* Wm. C. Brown Publishers, Dubuque.

Covell, Charles V. 1984. *A Field Guide to Moths: Eastern North America.* Peterson Field Guide Series. Houghton Mifflin Co., New York.

Danks, Hugh V., editor. 1978. *Canada and Its Insect Fauna.* Memoirs of the Entomological Society of Canada, No. 108.

Dunn, Gary A. 1996. *The Insects of the Great Lakes Region.* University of Michigan Press, Ann Arbor.

Gordon, Robert. 1985. *The Coccinellidae (Coleoptera) of America North of Mexico. Journal of the New York Entomological Society*, Volume 93, Number 1.

Handfield, Louis. 1999. *Le guide des papillons du Québec*. Broquet, Ottawa.

Holland, W.J. 1968. *The Moth Book*. Dover Publications Inc., New York.

Holmes, A.M., Q.F. Hess, R.R. Tasker and A.J. Hanks. 1991. *The Ontario Butterfly Atlas*. Toronto Entomologists' Association/D.W. Friesen, Altona, Manitoba.

Jaques, H.E. 1980. *How to Know the Beetles*, 2nd ed. Wm. C. Brown Publishers, Dubuque, Iowa.

Kaston, B.J. 1978. *How to Know the Spiders. Pictured Key Nature Series*. Wm. C. Brown Publishers, Dubuque.

Layberry, Ross, Peter W. Hall and J. Donald Lafontaine. 1998. *The Butterflies of Canada*. University of Toronto Press. Toronto.

Leonard, Jonathan, and Ross T. Bell. 1999. *Northeastern Tiger Beetles: A Field Guide to Tiger Beetles of New England and Eastern Canada*. CRC Press, New York.

Lindroth, Carl H. 1961–69. *The Ground-beetles of Canada and Alaska. Opuscula Entomologica Supplementa XX, XXIV, XXIX, XXXIII, XXXIV and XXXV.*

Needham, James G., Minter J. Westfall and Michael L. May. 2000. *Dragonflies of North America*. Revised Edition. Scientific Publishers, Gainesville.

Opler, Paul A., and Vichai Malikul. 1998. *A Field Guide to Eastern Butterflies*. The Peterson Field Guide Series. Houghton Mifflin. New York.

Otte, Daniel. 1981. *North American Grasshoppers*. Volume 1. Harvard University Press.

———. 1984. North American Grasshoppers. Volume 2. Harvard University Press.

Pyle, Robert Michael. 1981. *The Audubon Society Field Guide to North American Butterflies*. Alfred A. Knopf, New York.

———. 1992. *Handbook for Butterfly Watchers*. Houghton Mifflin Co., Boston and New York.

Rockburne, Eric W., and Donald Lafontaine. 1976. *The Cutworm Moths of Ontario and Quebec*. Research Branch, Canada Department of Agriculture. Publication 1593, 1976.

Shaw, John. 1987. *John Shaw's Closeups in Nature: The Photographer's Guide to Techniques in the Field*. AMPHOTO, New York.

Wagner, David L., Valerie Giles, Richard C. Reardon and Michael L. McManus. *Caterpillars of Eastern Forests*. United States Department of Agriculture.

Walker, Edmund M. 1953. *The Odonata of Canada and Alaska*. Volume 1. The University of Toronto Press, Toronto.

———. 1958. *The Odonata of Canada and Alaska*. Volume 2. The University of Toronto Press, Toronto.

Walker, Edmund M., and Philip S. Corbet. 1975. *The Odonata of Canada and Alaska*. Volume 3. The University of Toronto Press, Toronto.

Westfall, Minter J., Jr., and Michael L. May. 1996. *Damselflies of North America*. Scientific Publishers, Gainesville, Florida.

Wheeler, George C., and Jeanette Wheeler. 1963. *The Ants of North Dakota*. University of North Dakota, Grand Forks.

White, Richard E. 1983. *A Field Guide to the Beetles of North America*. Peterson Field Guide Series. Houghton Mifflin Co., New York.

Yanega, Doug. 1996. *Field Guide to the Northeastern Longhorned Beetles (Coleoptera: Cerambycidae)*. Illinois Natural History Survey, Champaign-Urbana, Ill.

# ORGANIZATIONS

In addition to the books, here is the contact information for various societies that can help you further your interest in bugs and enhance your enjoyment of the subject. Some are local, and some are worldwide, but all have publications and meetings.

American Arachnological Society: c/o Norman I. Platnick, Membership Secretary. Department of Entomology, American Museum of Natural History, Central Park West at 79th Street, New York, New York, 10024-5192.
Website: http://americanarachnology.holycross.edu/

Coleopterists' Society: contact the society's treasurer, currently Terry Seeno, CDFA-PPD, 3294 Meadowview Road, Sacramento, California, 95832-1448, U.S.A.
E-mail: tseeno@ns.net
Website: http://www.coleopsoc.org/

Dragonfly Society of the Americas: c/o T. Donnelly, 2091 Partridge Lane, Binghamton, New York. 13903, U.S.A.
Website: http://www.afn.org/~iori/dsaintro.html
E-mail: YESbugs@aol.com
E-mail: 72737.3624@compuserve.com

Entomological Society of Canada: 1320 Carling Avenue, Ottawa, Ontario, K1Z 7K9.
Website: http://www.biology.ualberta.ca/esc.hp/homepage.htm

Entomological Society of Ontario. c/o Barry Lyons, Secretary. Canadian Forestry Service, 1219 Queen Street East. Sault Ste. Marie, Ontario, P6A 2E5.

Lepidopterists' Society: c/o Los Angeles County Museum, 900 Exposition Boulevard, Los Angeles, California, 90007-4057, U.S.A.
Website: http://www.furman.edu/~snyder/snyder/lep/

Toronto Entomologists' Association. c/o Alan Hanks, Treasurer, 34 Seaton Drive, Aurora, Ontario, L4G 2K1.
Website: http://members.aol.com/yesbugs/bugclub.html

Young Entomologists' Society: 1915 Peggy Place, Lansing, Michigan, USA, 48910-2553.

*And finally, for entomological supplies and/or books, you can contact the following:*
Bio Quip Inc.: 17803 LaSalle Avenue, Gardena, California, USA, 90248-3602.
Phone: (310) 324-0620, fax (310) 324-7931.
E-mail: bioquip @aol.com.

Jean Paquet: 3 rue du Coteau, P. O. Box 953, Pont Rouge, Québec, Canada, G3P 2E1.
E-mail: jeanpaquet@webnet.qc.ca.

# INDEX

Page numbers in **boldface** type refer to the primary, illustrated accounts.

# ABOUT THE AUTHOR

Since the age of five, John Acorn has been hopelessly fascinated by insects—a benign affliction that eventually led to a Master's degree in Entomology. His thesis work focused on tiger beetles, which are still among his favourite insects. Today, he works as an award-winning freelance writer, speaker and broadcaster, and he is best known as "Acorn, The Nature Nut," host of an international television series that appears on *The Discovery Channel*. John spends most of his spare time being exactly what you might expect—a bugster. He is also the author of several of Lone Pine's best-selling nature guides.

# ABOUT THE ILLUSTRATOR

Ian Sheldon has been captivated by bugs since the age of three. Born in Canada, Ian later lived in South Africa, England and Singapore. Exposure to nature from so many different places enhanced his desire to study bugs and other creatures further, and he earned an award from the Zoological Society of London and a degree from Cambridge University. He has also completed a Master's degree in Ecotourism Development. Ian is an accomplished artist represented by galleries internationally, and he is both a writer and illustrator of many other nature guides, including Lone Pine's *Seashore of Northern and Central California* and *Animal Tracks of Ontario*.